UNWAVERING

Love and Resistance in WW2 Germany
Book 3

Marion Kummerow

UNWAVERING

Love and Resistance in WW2 Germany, Book 3

Marion Kummerow

All Rights Reserved

Copyright © 2017 Marion Kummerow

Cover Design by http://www.StunningBookCovers.com

Cover Photo: Bundesarchiv, Bild 183-J30142 / CC-BY-SA 3.0 https://creativecommons.org/licenses/by-sa/3.0/de/deed.en

Table of Contents

Chapter 1

November 30, 1942

Hilde Quedlin repeatedly glanced at the clock on the sideboard while she sat on the floor playing with her children. Three-year-old Volker played with wooden blocks handed down from his aunts while nine-month-old Peter relentlessly tried to balance on his hands and knees. He was so close to crawling, and Hilde's heart filled with pride and joy as she watched both of her little sunshines.

Worry seeped into her. Today, Q had met the Russian agent after work and should be coming back any minute. Time crawled as she prayed for her husband's safe return home.

She sniffed the distinctive smell of a full diaper and huddled Peter in her arms to carry him to the nursery. The little man was less than enthusiastic to be disturbed in his crawling exercises and kicked his little feet against his mother.

Hilde laughed. "Easy, little man. I'll let you down again when you're clean and fresh."

When she returned to the living room, she glanced

at the clock again. *Why hasn't Q returned?* It usually didn't take that long.

A sharp knock on the door interrupted her worries. He'd probably forgotten his keys. She settled Peter on her hip and patted Volker's head as she passed him to open the door.

It wasn't Q.

Fear gripped her at the sight of two officers in long black leather coats. Gestapo.

"*Frau* Quedlin?" one of them asked.

Her voice failed, and she could only nod.

"You are under arrest."

Despite the baby warming her, the blood chilled in her veins. "What? Why? I don't understand..." Hilde said, terror in her voice.

"All will be explained to you, but you must come with us now." The younger officer said, his dead steel blue eyes seeming to look through her.

"No, please...my children. There is no one else here to watch them," Hilde pleaded and pressed Peter tighter against her. He didn't like the treatment and kicked to be sat down.

The senior Gestapo officer looked at the little boy. With straight, light-brown hair and blue eyes, he was the spitting image of his mother, and Hilde thought she saw a glimpse of compassion in the officer's eyes, but she could have been wrong.

At that moment, Volker came rushing from the living room and froze in his tracks at the sight of the black-coated men. He clung onto Hilde's skirts and peeked around her knees. Volker was the epitome of an Aryan child. Hilde had let his hair grow, and his white-blond curls framed his pale skin and bright blue eyes in the cutest way possible. When he grew into a man, he would look exactly like his father.

"They'll be taken to the children's ward," the younger officer said, dissolving her illusion of leniency.

"No, please...let me call my mother..." Hilde's heart stopped at the notion of their little sunshines fending for themselves in some orphanage.

"Call her," the older officer said, silencing the protest of the other one. "We can search the place while we wait." He stepped into the foyer, causing Hilde to stumble back, and she watched in growing horror as three more officers rushed inside and began opening the drawers and cupboards, rummaging without care through the contents.

"Please, what is this about? My husband is–"

The younger officer turned on her. "Your husband has already been arrested. Make your call."

Hilde swallowed hard and ushered Volker into the kitchen. With shaking hands, she placed Peter in his high chair.

"Mama?" Volker shrieked, watching with wide

eyes as the Gestapo officers ransacked the house.

"Shush. It will be okay, Volker. Mama's calling grandma to come stay with you for a bit. Won't that be fun?" Hilde picked up the phone and dialed her mother's number with trembling fingers. A stone fell from her heart when Annie answered on the third ring.

"Annie Klein."

"Mother, it's Hilde. I need you to come stay with the children. Please...the Gestapo is here and say I must go with them." Hilde's voice was wobbly, and she had to lean against the wall to steady herself.

"The Gestapo? What have you done this time?" Annie wanted to know, her voice accusatory, causing Hilde to flinch.

"Nothing, there must be some mistake. Please, could you come right away?" She hated to ask her mother for this favor. Annie was probably the least suitable person to take care of the two active boys, but who else would rush to her house with the Gestapo present?

"I do have to get ready to go to the opera tonight, but I guess I could cancel it and come over."

"You have no idea how much this means to me..." Hilde sighed. At least her children would be safe.

"I'm not doing this for you, but for my grandchildren." Annie gave an annoyed sound. "I thought your days of troublemaking had stopped when you got married."

Hilde chose not to argue with her mother. "I will tell them you are on your way. Thank you."

But Annie was gone. She'd hung up the phone without responding or offering her daughter a word of reassurance. When Hilde looked up, the senior Gestapo officer was standing in the kitchen, watching her with narrowed eyes.

"My mother is on her way. She doesn't live far away, and it will take fifteen or twenty minutes..." Her voice strangled as emotion closed her throat like a vice.

"Fine. We will wait for her arrival."

Hilde nodded and rushed to Peter, who had started wailing from his chair. She picked the frightened child up, and his little arms wrapped around her neck. "Shush, Mama's here."

The senior officer continued to observe her with cold eyes, giving Hilde the chills. Her heart was beating an erratic rhythm until she'd gathered enough courage to address him.

"Please, can you tell me what's happening? Why am I being arrested? Why was my husband arrested?" Her eyes searched the face of the officer for an emotion, anything. But it was as animated as a marble statue.

"You will be informed of the charges against you once we arrive at the Prinz-Albrecht-Strasse 8."

The breath stuck in her lungs even as cold sweat broke out on her palms. Hilde hugged her baby tight. *Gestapo Headquarters.* The words reverberated through her body, sending tremors into every limb. The ornate building looked nice enough on the outside, but everyone had heard the rumors about what went on inside the three-story stone building. Horrible visions filled her mind, and an icy hand grabbed at her heart. It was all she could do not to break down in tears.

"Mama, I'm hungry," Volker whined, coming to lean against her knees where she sat.

Hilde brushed a hand over his head and hugged him close. "Grandma Annie will be here soon, and I will have her get you something to eat, okay?"

Volker was such a good little boy, and he nodded, turning to look at the Gestapo officer in silence. Hilde wanted to hide her children away from the horror that she feared was to come into their lives, but she was powerless to do so.

Fifteen minutes later, her mother swept into the kitchen, a look of incredulity on her face. "Hilde, what is the meaning of this?"

"Mother, I-"

Annie turned away from her daughter and addressed the Gestapo officer with her brightest smile. "*Kommissar*, I'm Annie Klein. My husband, the opera singer Robert Klein, and I are devoted fans to our great *Führer*. Hitler has more than once graced the performances of my husband with his presence. I'm awfully sorry for the inconvenience my daughter has caused. She was always a troublemaker. It's her father's fault. He left us when she was still a baby. I was so young..." Annie dabbed a tear from her eye and put a hand over her heart before she continued, "...it will always lie on my conscience that my own daughter wouldn't follow the path of virtue like any good German woman should. But rest assured, I will make sure the same won't happen with my grandsons. They're in good hands with me."

Hilde stared at Annie, anger exploding through her at the blatant lies her mother was telling. It wasn't her father who had left. He'd been a soldier in the trenches of the Great War. Her mother had eloped with her soon-to-be second husband, the glamorous opera singer Robert Klein, and dumped two-year-old Hilde on the doorstep of Annie's mother-in-law.

The Gestapo officer waved his hand. "Let's go."

Hilde's breath caught in her throat, and she found that she was unable to move even if she'd wanted to.

"Go with him," Annie urged and shoved her out of the kitchen, taking a screaming Peter from her arms. "We'll be fine, won't we?"

"Thank you, Mother," Hilde croaked, glancing back at her children while she forced her feet to take one step after another away from them.

Chapter 2

Q's entire body was itching with anxiety. The Gestapo had taken all his personal belongings, including his watch, and then shoved him into an interrogation room before they disappeared. The room was empty except for a rickety metal table and two worn out wooden chairs. Q sat down and stared at the grey stone wall.

For a while, he counted the seconds to keep track of time and take his mind off what was to come. But that hadn't helped him find some semblance of calm. Neither had pondering on a tricky scientific problem. Nor holding onto the thought that even the Gestapo couldn't prove Hilde was involved. Despite his efforts to block out the reality, angst seeped into his bones. Agonizing, strangling terror.

Q had lost count of the minutes and hours when the door finally opened with a bone-chilling creak, and a senior Gestapo officer stepped inside. By now, he didn't care anymore. Anything was better than sitting in the empty room, waiting for the worst, and letting his imagination run wild.

"I am *Kriminalkommissar* Becker. You are in very severe trouble."

"What are the charges against me?" Q hoped the *Kriminalkommissar* didn't hear the cracks in his voice.

Kriminalkommissar Becker shook his head. "I ask the questions, not you. You are an intelligent man, so you know it's in your best interest to answer them quickly and honestly." Becker slammed his hands on the table and leaned forward. "Let's begin. State your full name."

Q took a breath. "Wilhelm Quedlin."

"Your age?"

"Thirty-nine."

"Are you married?"

Q lifted a questioning eyebrow. "Yes, but you know that already."

"Answer my questions," Becker snapped, his voice hardened as his steel grey eyes clearly showed his annoyance.

"Your wife's name?"

"Hildegard Quedlin. Born Dremmer." Q fought the impulse to jump up and ask Becker how long these stupid questions would continue. If they didn't already know this information, everyone gave too much credit to the Gestapo. Why did Becker waste time asking non-relevant stuff?

"Where do you work?"

Q's jaw clenched at yet another stupid question. "I work at Loewe Radio Technologies."

"And what do you do at Loewe?" Becker's grey eyes pierced Q in place, which told Q that they were finally getting somewhere.

"I work with the radio transmitters and research." Q tried to answer as truthfully as possible without giving away anything the *Kriminalkommissar* didn't already know.

Becker pulled out a packet of papers from a briefcase and threw them on the table. "You gave these papers to an agent."

"I don't know what you mean. What agent?" Q's heart thumped in his throat as he recognized the blueprints he'd given to Gerald a while ago. *Oh God, they must have caught him, too.*

"You don't recognize these papers?" The *Kriminalkommissar* smirked and pushed the papers across the table.

Q thumbed through them, the chill seeping deeper into his bones as each page revealed itself. What lay before him was the entire collection of intelligence he'd given to Gerald over the last two months. Some of them had been typewritten, but many drawn by hand – Q's hand – and some included handwritten comments. There was no sense in denying they were his work.

"On a second glance, I do recognize some of them," Q said, feverishly thinking about his next move. How much did Becker know?

For a moment, a cruel smile flickered on Becker's lips. "Good. And how did they get into the hands of the agent?"

"How should I know?" Q challenged Becker.

Becker gave Q a nonchalant smile. "Look. I've been friendly with you so far, but I can easily change that. Do you want me to call in my men?" The question was as indifferent as his facial expression. He might have been asking about the weather instead of threatening torture.

Q shook his head, swallowing down the rising fear. "No."

"Who is the man you gave the papers to?" Becker demanded, seemingly uninterested as he inspected his fingernails.

Q decided to give Becker what he wanted. His own life was probably not worth a single *Pfennig* anymore, but he could at least try to protect Gerald. "He was a Russian agent and called himself Pavel."

"Pavel, is it? Any last name by chance?" Becker leaned across the table, his cold eyes fixated on Q's.

Q felt like a rabbit staring at a snake, but shrugged casually. "No. Sorry. He never mentioned his last name."

Without warning, Becker jumped up and knocked the table over until the hard edge pressed into Q's lap. Becker leaned on his edge of the metal plate, and Q winced but refused to give the *Kriminalkommissar* the satisfaction of crying out in pain.

"You're lying," Becker snapped, his lip curled in disgust, adding more of his weight on the table.

"No...ahh...he said to call him Pavel," Q forced out the words, and the pressure on his thighs subsided slightly. "He was very careful not to tell me anything compromising."

"Didn't it strike you as strange that your *Russian* Pavel wasn't a Russian at all?" Becker asked, his voice once again conversational.

Q's fingers dug into his legs. The Gestapo knew everything about Gerald. He wasn't to be saved anymore, but Q decided to stick with the Pavel-version.

"Not Russian?" Q shook his head, his face a mask of confusion. "Now that you mention it, I remember thinking his German was flawless. He must be one of the Volga Germans."

Becker put the table back on its four legs and changed the topic. "Do you confess to the crime of spying on the Party?"

"No." Q pointed at the papers that had fallen to the floor. "I merely gave technical information to a country that used to be our Ally."

A warning light flickered in Becker's eyes, and Q understood the message. He needed to play by Becker's rules if he wanted to get out of this interrogation alive.

"That's called high treason," Becker said with a smug smile on his face that widened as he noticed the fear spreading across Q's. "For how long have you done this hideous crime?"

It probably wouldn't make any difference to his sentence, but if he told him he'd been in contact with the Soviet trade mission since before Hitler's *Machtergreifung* ten years ago, the Gestapo would investigate every single person he'd had contact with during the last decade. Johanna and Reinhard from the communist literature club. His friends Leopold, Otto, and Jakob. No, not him. Jakob was dead. Killed by the Brownshirts. Every single engineer and scientist he'd shared information with. His colleagues at the Botanical Reichs Institute. His patent lawyer. Harro Schulze-Boysen. Erhard Tohmfor. Martin Stuhrmann. Hilde. He needed to protect them at all costs.

"A year, give or take a few months," Q hedged.

Becker's nostrils flared. "Give me the names of everyone else involved."

Q shook his head, giving him his most earnest look. "I worked alone."

"That is a lie. Your wife helped you."

Q gasped. The seeping chill in his bones intensified. *Not Hilde.* "No! She would never. She's innocent. My wife has no idea of my actions. She would never approve. It was all my own doing."

Kriminalkommissar Becker didn't respond. Instead, he stood and retrieved one of the scattered papers from the floor. He scrutinized it, as if intently interested in its contents. Q had a sense of foreboding. A very bad foreboding.

"There are no corrections on this sheet. Do you know how to type this well?" *Kriminalkommissar* Becker tapped the documents in front of him.

Q shook his head. He was a dismal typist. "It is true that my wife often typed the information I needed, both for my patents and for my intelligence work. But, as you can see, those are complex technical documents, and she had no idea of their meaning. I always let her believe it was a technical description I needed for my research."

A rap on the door interrupted their conversation. Q wasn't sure if he should be relieved or more frightened.

"*Herein,*" Backer called out, and another Gestapo officer peeked inside, making a gesture Q couldn't decipher. Becker nodded in response, then scooped up the papers and walked to the door. Just before stepping into the hallways, he turned. "Doctor Quedlin, I said this at the beginning of our little chat, and I will say it again. You are in severe trouble. The way I see it, you'll be accused of high treason and receive the death sentence."

Q's mouth went dry. He knew the punishment for treason, and he'd been expecting it for such a long time, he thought he'd come to terms with the prospect of such a sentence. But hearing it from Becker's mouth was totally different than imagining it in his own mind.

I want to live!

Becker stood in the doorway, closely observing Q's struggle with that prospect before he spoke again. "But I'm no monster. You are an intelligent man, and I'm sure you'll see the benefits of my offer. If you agree to work with us and give us the names of everyone involved in your subversive work, I will see that you receive a mild punishment. Or none at all."

The door closed with a creak, and Q's mind raced with a million thoughts. Here was his chance to save his life. This interrogation had been short and easy. The next one wouldn't.

A short time later, two officers stepped into the little room and escorted Q to a holding cell. They shoved him inside and slammed the door shut. Q gazed at the empty five by eight feet space that was now his. The ceiling hung barely above his head. It reminded him of an oversized closet, and he wondered how long he would be kept here before they moved him or…killed him.

The cell was completely made of stone and brick, the walls a dull grey. Previous prisoners had scratched or painted the walls, no doubt in the quest to leave some bit of evidence of their existence and suffering.

A shiver ran down Q's spine. Reluctantly, he sat on the corner of a blood-stained mattress lying on the floor. A rough woolen blanket was the only dressing on the mattress – no sheets or pillow. He looked away from the stinking bucket standing in one corner. Q forced down the bile rising in this throat and closed his eyes.

When he was certain he wouldn't throw up, he opened them again and inspected his cell more closely, peering into the dimness surrounding him. There was a small window with iron bars over the glass, but the glass was opaque and would only let in a small amount of light when the sun shone. A single bulb hung from the ceiling, but it was switched off. This time of year, it got dark around four-thirty in the evening, and he had no means to estimate the time that had passed since his arrest.

Judging by the rumbling of his stomach, it was past midnight by now. The guards had thoughtfully left a bowl with an undefined, stinking liquid on the corner opposite to the bucket, but he wasn't hungry enough to force it down – yet. He had no doubt, though, that in a few days from now he'd be gratefully devouring whatever food arrived.

Chapter 3

Hilde sat in the car, squeezed between two Gestapo officers. Despite the chilly November day, she was sweating. The air was too thick to breathe and pure panic tied up her throat.

The car passed the familiar streets and places of Berlin, but she had no eye for them. Neither for the natural beauties of Nikolassee where she lived, nor for the erstwhile majestic art nouveau buildings that had been reduced to rubble – skeletons rising into the sky as a reminder of the harrowing war raging across the world.

Hilde's limbs were numb with fear when the car arrived at Gestapo Headquarters, and she was shoved into the building. Inside the dreary interrogation room, she was left alone. Paralyzed with fear, she plopped down on one of the two chairs and lifted a hand to her chest. She clasped the red jasper pendant on the gold necklace Q's mother had given her for their wedding. *This is the lucky stone for your zodiac sign*, Ingrid had said. Hilde could use some luck now, although luck alone wouldn't be enough. She would need a lot of strength and endurance to bear what was to come.

The door opened, and a Gestapo officer walked in and shut the door with a long creak. *"Frau* Quedlin, I am *Kriminalkommissar* Becker."

Hilde inclined her head, trying to hide her fear. *Kriminalkommissar* Becker took a seat opposite her at the metal table and leaned back in his chair. He could be called handsome, with his broad shoulders, short blond hair, and classic features, if it wasn't for his soulless grey eyes.

Becker observed her for a few minutes and suddenly smiled what seemed to be a genuine smile. Hilde felt the fear easing out of her system. Maybe the rumors were highly exaggerated, and this wouldn't be as bad as she imagined. If she could convince him that she was innocent, he might even let her return to her children.

"I have a few questions to begin with. Could you please state your name, including your maiden name?" Becker's voice was pleasant, friendly even.

Hilde nodded. "Hildegard Quedlin. Born Dremmer."

"Age and place of birth."

"Thirty. I was born in Hamburg on August 23, 1912." Hilde focused on answering his questions, suppressing the tremble in her voice.

"You are married to Wilhelm Quedlin?"

"Yes, *Herr Kriminalkommissar.*"

"Do you have children?"

Hilde cast her eyes down, the thought of her two precious babies bringing tears to her eyes. "I have two sons. Nine months and three years old."

"Could you find someone to care for them right now?" Becker asked, showing an empathetic smile.

Hilde met his grey eyes and believed she saw a spark of compassion, but it disappeared as quickly as it had arrived. She willed her tears away and said softly, "I was allowed to call my mother. She's with them now."

"That must be a relief for you," Becker said and leaned forward. Hilde shivered. Despite the polite, even friendly, manners this man emitted bad vibes.

She nodded. "Yes."

"Your husband was arrested earlier today and will most likely be accused of treason. What do you have to say to that?" Becker launched his question without prior warning.

Hilde caught her breath. *Treason?* She knew what that meant. Q had warned her about the consequences, but she'd always believed such a thing would only happen to other people, not to them. They'd been careful. They wouldn't be caught.

"I...don't understand. My husband is a good man, a good citizen."

Becker sat up tall and pierced her with his steel gray eyes. *He doesn't believe me.*

"*Frau* Quedlin, you don't strike me as being

stupid. In fact, I would venture to say you are more intelligent than most women. It would be in your best interest to tell me everything you know about your husband's subversive activities. Who he met with. How long this has been going on. How he makes contact with them. Everything."

"*Kriminalkommissar*, I'm as shocked as you are. This must be a misunderstanding. My husband is a gentle man–"

Becker slammed his hand down on the table, making her jump. "Who has been working with the resistance! And if you thought for one minute about your two sons you'd tell me everything you know."

"I don't know anything." Hilde shook her head. "If he really worked against our government, which I doubt, he never told me. He was devoted to his work, making radio transmitters for the Wehrmacht. He's not a spy." The lies came easy enough.

Becker scowled at her, then withdrew some of the papers she'd typed for Q and slid them across the table to her. "Do you deny typing these?"

Hilde looked at the papers and inwardly cringed. Despair took hold of her. She steeled her spine and stuck to her story. "I've never seen those papers before."

"You are denying that you deliberately tried to disguise the typewriter these directions were written on? You are denying that you were the person operating the typewriter?"

"Yes." She nodded fervently.

"Do you have a typewriter at your home, *Frau* Quedlin?"

"Yes." Hilde's mind whirled, and she had difficulties following the staccato of Becker's questions.

"Do you know how to type?"

"Yes."

"And is it not true that you often helped your husband by typing up his research and documentation for his patents?"

"Yes, but I don't understand where this is going."

"And is it not true that you assisted him in copying secret and confidential documents, using blueprint and brown paper to distort the letters, making identifying the typewriter much more difficult?"

"I have typed things for him on blueprint paper, but not...I haven't done anything wrong. My husband likes to make copies of his research, and he would dictate, and I would type. I never understood the technical contents of what I was typing. And surely, he would never copy secret and confidential material-"

Becker slammed his fist on the metal table again. The screeching sound curled Hilde's toes. "Stop babbling."

Hilde nodded, her eyes wide open. She expected

him to hit her and was grateful when he leaned back and apologized.

"Please forgive my manners, *Frau* Quedlin. But I hate being lied to. And you are lying."

"I haven't done anything wrong," she protested.

"You need to come up with a better story than that. Preferably the truth. This could be smooth and easy. You could be back with your children in no time at all. Or..."

Her blood froze in her veins.

Becker slid the papers back to his side of the table and stood up. "Well, maybe you just need some time to think about things." He opened the door and called two junior officers into the room. "Take *Frau* Quedlin to her cell. She requires more time to think about the truth. *Frau* Quedlin, I will see you tomorrow."

Chapter 4

Q was alone in his cell, which was a surprise. He'd heard about ten to twenty prisoners being crowded into spaces as small as this one. While companionship might have been nice, he was actually thankful for the opportunity to think.

For ten years, he'd been waiting for this moment, fearing how his life might end if his resistance efforts were ever found out. The fear had always been present in the back of his mind. Every time he'd sabotaged the war production at Loewe, stolen another piece of intelligence, or met with the Russian agent, his life had been a catastrophe waiting to happen.

At least this constant worry was gone now. A tiny trace of relief took hold of him before the far-reaching consequences of his capture shattered all sense of relief, and a different kind of fear took hold of him. The certainty of torture and agony gripped him like the cold hand of death.

But death wasn't cruel like the Gestapo bloodhounds were, and Q was sure that at some point in the near future, he'd welcome death as salvation from his torment. Despite Becker's friendly façade, Q had seen the determined gleam in his gray eyes. The determination to get what he wanted, at all cost, by all means necessary. If only men like Becker would put their unwavering determination to a worthwhile cause and not destroy their fellow humans.

Q shuddered. *Kriminalkommissar* Becker had offered him a deal. Promised a mild punishment, a release, if Q worked with the Gestapo. The only thing he had to do was confess to his activities and rat out everyone else. It was the easy way out, and Q was more than tempted to take it.

But he couldn't do that to his friends. Have them pay for his deeds? No. How would he be able to live his life as a traitor? A true traitor who betrayed his own ideals, not some despicable government. And what if this was just a ploy to get him to talk?

No, Q wouldn't fall for their tactics. In the solitude of his cell, his will was strong. If that would hold true during his next interrogation, he didn't know. *I'm not a hero. Not a soldier trained to endure pain. I'm just a scientist. An ordinary man.*

How could he ensure he didn't betray his friends when the Gestapo came back for him? Q relaxed on the stinking mattress and did what he knew best: think. He devised a plan.

He would tell the Gestapo everything they wanted to know. Every little detail about his sabotage work at Loewe. How he'd copied the blueprints and given them to "Pavel." He'd talk so much, *Kriminalkommissar* Becker wouldn't have the time to ask about names. Because names he wouldn't tell. Those he'd take to his grave.

Hilde.

Q's heart grew weary. Images appeared in his mind. Their wedding day. Climbing Mount Etna. Holding Volker for the first time. Sadness choked his throat. Would he ever see her and his sons again?

He hoped she was safe. She was just a woman, a mother. Not even the Gestapo could believe she had something to do with his resistance activities.

Q listened into the silence. All he could hear was a distant shuffling. Other prisoners? Gestapo coming for him? The shuffling stopped. Judging by the small, opaque window near the ceiling of his cell, he was in the cellar of the building. The infamous Gestapo cellar? Q willed his mind to go down another road, but the threat of what was to come kept him circling back.

What happened to Gerald?

Kriminalkommissar Becker had been in possession of some of the paperwork Q had given the agent the last time they'd met. Gerald was a *Wehrmacht* deserter, and everyone knew what happened to them if they got caught.

Fear and cold crept into his bones. Sleep was impossible, and Q stood up to pace the tiny cell.

Walk and think. Had he made the right choices in his life? Should he have stopped his subversive work? Not planned the attack on Goebbels? Never married Hilde? A thousand questions assaulted him. But no answers.

Much later that night, when he sank onto the mattress again and wrapped his freezing body with the rough blanket, his last thought was that he'd do everything again.

***

Hilde sat in a cell very similar to Q's, thinking about the horrific events that she now thought of as *Fateful Monday*. After the interrogation, they'd taken her down a narrow stairwell, into one of those clammy and moldy basements that always reminded her of a medieval dungeon.

Goosebumps rose on her skin. After the uniformed man shoved her inside and closed the door, the silence became deafening. The window was barred and opened into a grey light well. Nobody would hear her cries. But she didn't cry. Not yet.

Hilde paced the confines of the small room, her arms wrapped around herself. She was grateful for the cardigan she'd grabbed when the Gestapo had arrived for her. It was cold in here. But she'd have frozen even in plain sunlight because of the fear and sorrow filling her heart.

Kriminalkommissar Becker told her that Q had been arrested, too. She'd assumed that all along, but having certainty had knocked the breath out of her lungs. Q would probably be held in the same building, and she willed herself to *sense* his presence. If he was nearby, she could tap into his strength and envision him holding her the way he'd done so many times in their eight years together.

It worked, and she calmed down – until images of her babies crept into her mind and tears started streaming down her cheeks. She'd weaned Peter just the week before, and for that she was thankful because it would be so much harder for both of them if she were still nursing him. But she missed snuggling him next to her as he went down for a nap. She missed talking with Volker and watching his mind work as he played with his toys.

She consoled herself with the fact that her mother was with them. Despite her differences with Annie, she'd take good care of her grandsons.

It's only for a few days at most.

Hilde plopped onto the mattress on the ground and wrapped a stained, stinking blanket around her to find some warmth. But sleep was elusive, and she lay there, remembering the good times she'd shared with her husband and children.

Two weeks earlier, the weather had been unseasonably warm, and she and Q had taken both boys to the park. Peter had giggled and babbled in his pram. Volker and Q had walked hand-in-hand, both shuffling their feet through the autumn leaves.

The little boy had fired a million why-questions at his father. *Why are the leaves falling from the trees? Why is it autumn? Where did the summer go?*

Hilde cried some more. Would they ever experience such a peaceful and happy outing again? She rolled over, allowing her tears to flow unchecked and prayed to God.

Please. Allow me the chance to leave this place and return to my children. Please let me live to raise them, so they don't have to grow up without a mother like I did.

She and Q had discussed this exact situation, and she knew what he expected her to do. She'd always waved it away, but now that the situation had arrived, she struggled with the prospect of betraying her own husband. Put all the blame on him. To save herself.

Sleep finally claimed her in the wee hours of the morning, but her dreams were plagued with visions of her next interrogation. *Kriminalkommissar* Becker had been nice enough, but she knew that was simply a façade designed to break her down.

Chapter 5

It was still dark outside when two Gestapo officers hauled Q from the mattress, waking him from a fitful sleep. He didn't even have the time to put his shoes on, and of course, there was no breakfast either. He followed them without complaining. It wouldn't help.

This time, they took him to a different interrogation room. One without a table and only a single chair placed in the center of the room with a bare light bulb hanging overhead. The men shoved him into the room and ordered him to sit in the chair. Q did as they requested, trying not to think about whatever was to come. His stomach growled, reminding him that he hadn't eaten in eighteen hours.

Kriminalkommissar Becker entered a few moments later, finishing a bun that smelled of ham. Q's stomach growled. Becker wiped his mouth with his hand and smiled at him. "Good morning, Doctor Quedlin. I trust you had a good night's sleep?"

Q remained quiet at the bait the *Kriminalkommissar* was throwing at him. Becker acknowledged his silence with a smirk and walked towards Q, circling around the chair. He came to stand behind him, and chills of anticipated agony rushed down Q's spine.

"Have you had a chance to reconsider your answers to yesterday's questions? Are you ready to tell me who you were working with?" the voice came from behind.

Q shook his head. "I worked alone. Nobody else knew what I was doing."

The next moment, Q hurled through the air and braced his arms to cover his head before it smacked against the cold stone floor. He blinked as his eyes watered and the metallic taste of blood filled his mouth.

"Get up," Becker said.

Q pushed himself back to his feet and sat in the chair once again, wiping the corner of his mouth with his hand. A streak of blood appeared.

Becker stroked his knuckles and approached Q until he towered over him, staring down at him with dead grey eyes. "Who are your partners?"

Q swallowed and answered again, "I worked alone. Nobody else knew what I was doing–"

"That's a lie! It would be in your best interest to cooperate with me."

"I'm willing to tell you anything about my subversive work." Q hedged, and when Becker agreed, he felt a slight reprieve in his terror and started to talk. About the blueprints, how he gave all his research to the Russians. Everything. He talked for such a long time, he almost fooled himself into believing Becker would be satisfied.

"Now, tell me who helped you."

"I worked alone," Q insisted and received another blow to his jaw. The pain dizzied him, and for a minute he saw red stars.

"Gerald Meier said differently," Becker said.

So, they'd caught the Russian agent. Q clung to the hope that Gerald hadn't mentioned Erhard's name. Thankfully, Gerald hadn't known about Hilde and Martin. At least those two were safe.

"You arrested him, too?"

"Yes, and your friend Erhard Tohmfor."

No. Not Erhard, too. Q yearned to know if Erhard was still alive, but he was too afraid to ask. His own survival looked dimmer by the minute. It was too late to cover for him. Erhard was not to be saved either way.

"Erhard Tohmfor was my friend," Q explained, meeting Becker's eyes. "I believe he might have known about my stealing intelligence and my sabotage acts but turned a blind eye to it. He was never actively involved."

This time, the end of a wooden bat connected with Q's back and doubled him over, forcing all the air from his lungs. Again and again. The agonizing pain exploded into black stars, and his breathing became rattling as he panted for air. He must have passed out because when he came to, his arms and legs were shackled to the chair and Becker towered over him with a cup of deliciously smelling coffee in his hand.

"Oh good, you're awake," Becker said with a smug grin. "Let me tell you something. My department arrested the agent you knew as Gerald six weeks ago."

Six weeks? Even with his damaged brain, Q knew this wasn't possible. *Kriminalkommissar* Becker was lying. Because if it was true...

"But how? I met him just last week..." Q whispered, making an attempt to clear the fog from his mind.

"Well, unlike you, this man made a wise choice." Becker stared down at him. "He agreed to act as a double-agent for us in exchange for his life."

This was surreal. Unbelievable. But probably the truth. Suddenly, the pieces of the puzzle fell into place. That's why Gerald had started to ask all those questions. And why he'd insisted on another meeting before the assassination attempt.

Q's entire worldview shattered with this revelation. A double agent. The feeling of betrayal hurt as much as the physical pain from Becker's beatings. The person he'd trusted to be a comrade for the same cause had betrayed everyone to save his own life. He swallowed hard, trying to hide his shock.

"You thought you could trust this Russian agent, but really..." Becker chuckled, his grin growing wider, "a man as smart as you...you should have known how treacherous the Russians are."

Rage mixed with hurt and pain, and before Q could stop himself, he blurted out, "Well, this agent was, in fact, a German, so you see that only goes to show how treacherous the Germans are."

Becker's fist shot out and caught Q on the right side of his face, just a few inches below his eye. Thanks to his cuffs, he didn't fall off the chair this time, but his vision grew blurry as his eye immediately swelled and his mouth filled with the metallic taste of blood.

"Remember, we are not stupid. Gerald has told us everything about you. Scum." Becker spat in Q's face. "He's given us all the information you shared with him on your long walks together. We know everything. We also know about Erhard's role in your little sabotage effort."

Q was still processing the information when Becker struck again.

"We arrested your wife yesterday. Let's hope she's more cooperative than you are." Becker bared his teeth in what was probably supposed to be a smile, and Q's heart squeezed.

Not Hilde.

Q looked up. "*Herr Kriminalkommissar*, my wife is

innocent. I never told her about my resistance work. She knows absolutely nothing. You must believe me. She is innocent in all of this."

Becker looked at him with a calculating eye. "Who else besides Erhard and your wife was working with you?"

"No one, I swear. It was just Erhard and myself. Hilde had no idea what she was typing. She's not a scientist. She couldn't know."

"I'm fed up with your lies," Becker said and waved at another man. "Take him away."

This time, they shoved him into a cell slightly bigger than the one he'd spent the first night in. This one, though, was crowded with at least ten other prisoners. None of them looked any better than Q probably did, but they moved around, groaning, to make space for the newcomer on the hard stone floor.

Q was terrified. *The preferential treatment has ended.*

Chapter 6

Hilde woke after a fitful sleep and stretched her cold and aching limbs. Muffled noises from the hallway outside her cell reached her ears, the first sign of other persons being held down here.

When the door opened half an hour later, she backed up against the protection of the wall and watched warily to see who'd come inside. A uniformed Gestapo officer waved his baton, pushed a tray inside with his foot and then left without a word.

Hilde waited until she heard the bolt on the door engage before inspecting what she assumed was breakfast. She gulped down the foul-smelling water, then suspiciously eyed the piece of bread and the bowl with an indefinable whitish mash. Even though her mind rebelled, her stomach reminded her that they'd conveniently forgotten to give her food last night.

She held her nose and forced down half of the disgusting mush. Then she chewed the hard as stone piece of bread, not knowing when she might be given a chance to eat again.

Before long, another officer arrived to deliver her

to *Kriminalkommissar* Becker. He was sitting at the table in what looked like the same room she had been interrogated in the day before. The officer who'd escorted her leaned against the wall behind her.

"Good morning, *Frau* Quedlin, I hope you were not too uncomfortable last night?" He smiled and gestured for her to take a seat.

Hilde shrugged. "When can I go home?"

Becker steepled his hands atop the table, his eyes never leaving her. "That depends entirely on you and your willingness to cooperate. I have two wonderful children myself; you must be missing your sons. Is it the first time they've spent the night without you?"

She barely could press out, "Yes," before her eyes watered at the thought of her two babies.

"It would be such a shame if they became orphans," Becker mused, seemingly more to himself than to her.

That remark hit her harder than a punch to her stomach. She must have made a groaning sound because Becker now smiled at her benevolently.

"Well, well, *Frau* Quedlin. I have a soft spot in my heart for children, and therefore will make you an offer. Give me the names of everyone involved with your husband and the resistance effort he was part of. Everyone. Even the people you only suspect to be against the government."

Here was her chance to go home to her children.

All she had to do was betray everyone she knew and name ten, twenty, or thirty people Becker could go after.

"Does that mean I can go home again?" she asked, her voice cracking.

"Possibly," Becker agreed and smiled again. But his smile never reached his soulless eyes. Hilde was sure he was lying. Even if he wasn't, could she live with her conscience if she did what he demanded?

"I would love to tell you, but I don't know anything or anyone. I didn't even know that my husband was engaged in this abhorrent behavior until yesterday." She tried to sound as honest as possible.

"Now, *Frau* Quedlin, that is not quite the truth. Let's talk about those papers you typed out for your husband." *Kriminalkommissar* Becker slid some additional papers across the table to her.

Hilde looked at the papers, several of them simple patent requests and mundane notes she'd typed up for Q's research. She saw no harm in identifying them and nodded. "I remember typing these, so yes, I typed these for my husband."

"For once, you're telling me the truth," Becker said and produced the papers he'd shown her the day before and placed them side by side. "These papers were typed on the same typewriter."

Hilde's heart fell.

"Now explain to me why you lied yesterday?"

"*Kriminalkommissar* Becker, I'm sorry. I didn't recognize the papers. I typed many things for my husband. He's horrible at working the machine and oftentimes brought his research notes home and asked me to type them up." She wanted to jump up and run away, which was a rather stupid notion, given that she was inside the best-guarded building in Berlin. "I'm just a simple mother of two children, and frankly, I never gave much thought to what I was typing. It was usually at the end of the day when I was tired from caring for the children and our home."

"Haven't you ever wondered why your husband brought such sensitive material home with him?" Becker demanded to know.

Hilde's neck hair stood on end. "I didn't think it was sensitive."

"Don't you know that it's a crime to steal classified material?" Becker thumped the table with his fist.

The table jumped as did Hilde.

"No, he wasn't stealing. It was all his own work," she defended Q.

"How do you know?" Becker asked.

"I...he is an honest person."

"An honest person? So why did he betray *Führer* and Fatherland then?"

Hilde shrugged. Whatever she said, it would be wrong.

Becker stood and walked around the table to put a hand on her shoulder. Her entire body stiffened. Then she felt his breath at her ear, and she closed her eyes.

"Do you love your husband, *Frau* Quedlin?"

"Yes."

The hand grabbed her chin and turned her face until she was forced to stare into his eyes. "Does he love you?"

Hilde nodded.

"And still, you want to make me believe you had no idea about his political opinions. That he hated the admirable ideas of our *Führer* and collaborated with our enemy? That he was a communist in his heart?"

Hilde moaned as the grip tightened. "Yes. I mean, no. I didn't know any of that."

"So why didn't you admit to typing those papers yesterday," Becker asked again, squeezing her chin harder.

"I already told you, I didn't recognize them." Becker moved away and her face burned. Her skin probably showed the marks of his hand.

"Now, let's keep with the truth, will you?" Becker breathed into her ear, both his hands moving across her shoulders to rest around her neck.

Hilde gagged in panic. "I...I don't know. I panicked. I thought maybe those papers had something to do with my arrest."

"So, you knew there was something wrong about those papers?" he asked again and tightened the grip around her neck. Hilde thought he'd strangle her. Her pulse throbbed erratically as her vision began to dim. She kicked with her legs, clawed with her hands. She was desperate for air. Then she was free again.

As she gulped in precious oxygen, Becker strolled to the other side of the table and sat down. He steepled his hands again. "Talk."

Terror held Hilde's mind in her grip, and she couldn't think of anything intelligent to say. "No...I never thought there was something wrong with the papers. But yesterday, when you told me that my husband was accused of treason, I panicked. I thought maybe those papers had something to do with it."

"And you deemed it wise to lie to the Gestapo? Don't you know we have the means to find out the truth?" The threat in his voice made her shudder.

"I'm sorry."

"So, what exactly was in those papers?"

"I don't know."

Becker waved his hand, and Hilde's arm was jerked behind her back, probably by the officer who'd leaned against the wall. She screamed in pain. The pressure increased and she screamed until Becker waved again, and she was free.

"The truth, *Frau* Quedlin."

She was sobbing and holding her sore shoulder, her words coming out on ragged exhales. "The truth is I never knew anything."

"I don't believe you. See this." Becker held out the piece of paper with blurred letters.

Hilde tried to hide her gasp, but it was too late. Becker had already noticed her reaction.

"You recognize that one, right?"

"Yes." She did. Very well. It was the piece of paper where Q had given her explicit instructions to use several layers of paper on top of each other. Q's words rang in her ears. *It's better that you don't know. You need to be able to say you had no knowledge about the technical stuff you were typing.*

"Why are you suddenly so nervous, when you had no idea what this was all about?" Becker smirked at her.

She was as good as dead. There was no sense in denying anymore. Her visceral reaction had given her away. Her brain was fried, and the pain still lingered in her arm, making her unable to form a clear thought.

"At the time I was typing it, I didn't think much of it because my husband was very peculiar with his inventions, but now after my arrest, it seemed suspicious to me."

"You admit that you were helping your husband in his traitorous activities against the Reich?" Becker's voice was friendly, but his next words stung. "You scummy whore."

Tears shot into her eyes. The lack of sleep and food, the constant interrogations, it had taken a toll on her ability to focus. "I don't. I...knew nothing. And I didn't do anything wrong."

"And still you paled when I showed you the papers, you piece of scum."

There had to be something to turn this situation around. Hilde racked her frightened mind for an excuse. Anything. "I thought, that maybe...my husband...some shady business...trying to sell his research to a competing company. A little cheating...but not treason...never...he was loyal."

Loyal to his convictions. Just not to the monster who's our Führer.

"Bullshit. You knew exactly what you were doing. Treason." Becker stared at her until she squirmed and then stated, "We have arrested Erhard Tohmfor."

Hilde caught her gasp, but tears pooled in her eyes, and she had to blink them away.

Becker was a well-trained interrogator and caught her tiny lapse. He pressed her for more answers,

"Was Tohmfor involved in your husband's traitorous activities?"

"He was his boss. An honest person."

"Was he a traitor as well?" Becker shouted.

"My husband isn't a traitor, and neither was Erhard!" she spat out and earned herself a slap to her face. She tasted blood on her lip as the heat exploded across her cheek.

"Your pig of a husband is the worst kind of traitor. And so are you. And Erhard Tohmfor. And who else? Give me names!"

Hilde started crying. She didn't care anymore if Becker hit her or not. Maybe it would be better if he believed she was about to have a breakdown.

"Who else do you associate with?"

She swallowed and panicked deep inside. *The Gestapo would already know this information, right? Or should she lie?* Going with her first thought, she opted for a middle way. "My best friend is Erika Huber, the daughter-in-law of the late *SS- Obersturmbannführer* Wolfgang Huber. We often come together so our children can play."

If *Kriminalkommissar* Becker was impressed by her connection to Wolfgang Huber, he didn't show it. Instead, he continued to ask the same questions over and over. Hilde stuck to her line of defense, that she hadn't known what she was typing, and never once mentioned Martin Stuhrmann's name. The person who'd helped her husband to prepare the assassination plan on Goebbels.

The questions had become friendly again, but Hilde wasn't fooled. Inside the man sitting across from her was a cruel and sadistic monster enjoying the horror he inflicted.

Chapter 7

Q slumped against the wall in a ball of misery. His right eye was partially swollen shut, and the bruise on his left cheekbone was throbbing with every breath. But after having looked at the other prisoners in his cell, he felt privileged.

As bad as he felt for himself, he worried about his wife and friends more. Hilde arrested. Erhard arrested. Q wondered if Martin was safe. So far, his name hadn't been mentioned. *This means they don't know about him.* Gerald hadn't known about his existence, and now Martin's destiny lay in the hands of his friends. Q would rather die than betray him, but he wasn't sure how long he'd be able to hold on to that plan...and whether Hilde and Erhard could do the same.

Hilde. My love. It's my fault she's here. I have fed her to the wolves, and because of me, she's suffering now. His heart was in a tight knot. If only he could save her.

Several hours later, the Gestapo came back for him. This time, they took him down a different hallway. Downstairs. While walking, he heard the cries of fellow prisoners, muffled by the thick stone walls. Some were merely the pitiful whimpering of a man pushed to his breaking point.

These sounds shook him to the core, and by the time he was pushed into a windowless room with a chair and a large tub of water, all he could do was keep his knees from knocking together. *Kriminalkommissar* Becker stood in the room with an evil grin on his face.

"Traitorous pig!" Becker attacked him right away, followed by a long torrent of abuse. As he protected himself the best he could, he learned that Gerald had told the Gestapo about the assassination attempt on Goebbels. The Gestapo had then searched his home and found several drawings, including one for a remote-controlled bomb.

"A remote controlled bomb? *Herr Kriminalkommissar*, such a thing does not exist." Q had decided to play dumb.

"We found the drawings for such a device in your apartment," Becker shouted.

"Merely an idea. My mind is always filled with ideas, but exactly how would a remote-control device work? What method of transmitting the signal would be used? One day such a device may exist, but for now, it is simply a figment of my imagination." Q's teeth were shattering with anxiety and pain, but he managed to keep his voice steady.

"Liar! So far, I've treated you with kid's gloves, but this will change if you don't cooperate." Becker turned and stormed from the room, the other officers joining him.

Q was alone with only the sounds of the tortured souls in the other interrogation rooms for company.

After a few minutes, Becker returned with the drawings. "These are yours?"

"Yes, those are mine. I am an inventor, *Herr Kriminalkommissar*. I am always dreaming up new and innovative gadgets. It is why my services were so valuable to the Loewe." Of course, he'd never shared this specific device with his employer.

"Do you deny planning to assassinate our propaganda minister, Goebbels?" Becker demanded, picking up a wicked looking stick with leather thongs attached to the end.

Q's eyes were fixated on the stick in Becker's hand while he tried to focus on answering the question. "I admit I thought about it. It was a mind game, though. Gerald and I tossed around some ideas. We pondered whether it would diminish the Reich's power and shorten the war, or not." The more Q talked, the more confident he became. "But without having access to a powerful bomb, or the mythical remote control device to detonate it with, it was simply a dream. There was no way to make it a reality."

Becker didn't look convinced, so Q continued speaking, "I'm a scientist. I'm always inventing things, in theory, but other people have to actually build them. My ideas stop when I put them down on paper."

"It is unfortunate that you insist on sticking to this story," Becker said and nodded toward the two officers who'd followed him into the room. They grabbed Q, dragged him to the tub of water, and tossed him in.

The impact with icy water took his breath away, and when he was finally able to inhale, Q was plunged beneath the water and held there until he felt his lungs would explode if he didn't take a breath. This torture continued for most of the day. The only relief he got was when *Kriminalkommissar* Becker would return and ask him the same questions, over and over again.

Q stuck to his story. Convinced they would continue with the same procedure whether he told him what they wanted to hear or not. And for once, he was speaking the truth. As far as he knew, there was no such bomb in existence yet, except for his own prototype, which Martin hopefully had destroyed by now. He'd heard rumors about this kind of powerful bomb being in the experimental stage, but nothing official.

Late in the afternoon, when Q had long ago lost feeling in his frozen limbs, and even his thoughts had become viscous, Becker pulled him one last time from the tub of water and repeatedly beat him with the leather thongs.

The strikes slashed his ice-cold skin and brought

sensation back into Q's body. Excruciating pain. Hot fire burned his skin even as he shivered and shook from the cold and pain that racked his body.

"Tell me what I want to know, and you can go," Becker said many hours later.

Q barely lifted his head and answered with a battered voice, "I've told you everything. I'm a scientist. That drawing was mine and mine alone. A dream that will never come to fruition."

Becker looked at Q's battered and bruised body and evidently decided that Q must be telling the truth. He shook his head, instructing the other officers to help him back to the chair. "We will assume you are telling the truth about the drawing."

The *Kriminalkommissar* paced the room and then turned with an evil smile, "It's a shame, really. A man as bright as you. You could have worked for the Reich and become rich and powerful. But you chose to squander your brilliance by working for the enemy."

"I never wanted money. I always wanted progress. Progress *for* the people, not against them."

The remark earned him another slash with the whip, and Q chose to keep his next words for himself. That he wanted later generations to think honorably of him, which was why he stood up against Hitler, the person he thought would bring doom to his beloved Fatherland Germany. *National Socialism isn't good for anyone except for Hitler himself.*

"By the way, your friend Tohmfor confessed. Everything." With these words, Becker left the room. Q was alone with the two brutes who'd taken pleasure in almost drowning him for hours on end. He feared the worst.

But nothing happened. They dragged him back to his cell, where he fell on top of several fellow prisoners. *I'm still alive*, was his last thought before he fell into fits and bursts of an exhausted sleep.

Chapter 8

Q's trial took place on December 18, 1942, less than three weeks after his arrest by the Gestapo. It wasn't held in the normal courtrooms, but as a *Geheime Kommandosache,* a secret trial. Q wasn't even allowed a lawyer to defend him.

It wasn't illegal because the Gestapo law of 1936 gave the organization carte blanche to operate outside of, around, and without any concern for the law. In fact, the SS officer and former head of legal affairs in the Gestapo, Werner Best, had once said, "As long as the police carry out the will of the leadership, it is acting legally."

Q was handcuffed to the seat of the accused while a judge resided on a high bench. *Kriminalkommissar* Becker and the double-agent, Gerald Maier, sat to his left. Behind his back, more than two dozen Gestapo officers and supporters filled the room.

His heart leapt when he saw Hilde entering the room, handcuffed and accompanied by a Gestapo officer. Q sought her eyes, and when she looked his way, his heart broke at the devastation visible on her face. A bruise on her sunken cheek testified to the abuse she'd endured, and he wanted to scream. Or at least to walk over, take her into his arms, and kiss the pain away. Her dress bagged on her, and that sparkling twinkle in her blue eyes he'd loved so much had disappeared.

From his place, he could glance at her out of the corner of his eye without turning his head. Throughout the trial, he exchanged glances with her, conveying his unconditional love. He hoped that by some miracle, she'd forgive him for the mess he'd gotten them into.

Various Gestapo officers testified and Q listened as the evidence against him was stacked up. Documents were presented, including the drawing for the remote-control bomb device, and testimony was given in regards to his planned assassination of Goebbels.

The judge finally called an end to the testimony and leveled an ice-cold stare at him. Q inwardly quaked beneath the man's gaze.

"Aufstehen Angeklagter!"

Q pushed himself to his feet, holding back the groan of pain from his beatings in the previous days. He braced a hand on the table in front of him for a moment, and then forced himself to stand tall. *I will not give them the pleasure of seeing me broken.*

"Doctor Quedlin, you are accused of treason against the Party. The evidence has been presented. What do you have to say for yourself?"

Q glanced at Hilde, who sent him a barely visible nod, and then back to the judge, "I am guilty of committing the acts of subterfuge that have been discussed here today, but I did it to fight a regime of injustice. I would do so again. I acted in line with my conscience, a conscience that abhors what the Reich has done to my Fatherland. I would go to any means if it meant ridding Germany of this evil."

The small courtroom erupted in shouts for his death and curses aimed at his person. The officer seated next to him stood and grabbed his arm tightly, promising retribution for those bold statements.

***

Hilde had listened in growing horror as the evidence against him was presented. Until this moment, she hadn't grasped the extent of the Gestapo's knowledge about Q's intelligence and sabotage activities. They had been watching him and many others for months before arresting them.

She didn't understand everything that was said, but apparently, the Gestapo believed that Q had been the head of a sabotage group at his company, while at the same time belonging to a much bigger resistance network they called the *Red Orchestra*. Dozens of members, including the well-known Air Force *Oberleutnant* Harro Schulze-Boysen, had been arrested and were now tried by the same court.

A sense of pride filled Hilde as she observed Q standing unbroken in the courtroom. In his eyes, she'd seen a sea of pain. She sought out his glance every so often, trying to make him understand that she didn't blame him. That she'd forgiven him, if there ever was something to forgive. *If only I could have a few moments to speak with him.* But rows of benches, bars, and handcuffs separated them.

Her pride about his unwavering steadfastness transformed into plain horror when he was asked to defend himself. Hilde pressed a hand over her mouth. Wasn't it outright stupidity to deliberately enrage the judge and the spectators? Wouldn't it have been better to admit but restrain from adding fuel to the fire? The ensuing uproar was deafening, and for a moment, she feared someone would kill Q right on the spot.

The judge slammed his gavel on the bench several times, yelling at the spectators to calm down. A deadly silence ensued. At the end of it, the judge pronounced his sentence.

"The defendant, Doctor Wilhelm Quedlin, is found guilty of treason against *Führer* and Fatherland. He is sentenced to death." The judge paused for a moment and then added, "Get this piece of trash out of my courtroom."

Q's sagging shoulders were the last thing Hilde saw before she sank down, hiding her face in her hands. Silent tears streamed down her cheeks. Both of them had known what the punishment for treason was, and that no resistor could hope for mercy from the government. But knowing it as a theoretical fact and hearing with her own ears that the man she loved was sentenced to death were two different things.

Her heart broke into a million pieces, leaving a hollow place behind.

Q was shoved towards the door, passing by her place. He was too far away to touch him, even if she stretched out her hand. He frantically turned his head, and she caught one last glimpse into his loving blue eyes. A powerful energy passed between them. She would stay strong. She still had her sons to care for.

Chapter 9

Hilde spent the next two days in a state of trance in her cell. Since Q's trial, she'd not been interrogated, and while she loathed *Kriminalkommissar* Becker and his constant abuse, the uncertainty of what was to come was almost harder to endure.

At first, the other women in her cell had tried to console her, but soon enough, had given up. Each woman had her own problems. Prisoners would come and go, and many of them were incapable of walking, eating, or even talking after yet another interrogation. It seemed as if no one was any worse off than anyone else.

Hilde slumped against the cold cement, huddled into a ball, crying until she'd used up all her tears. Three weeks in the hands of the Gestapo and no end in sight. She hadn't been allowed a lawyer or a visitor. Hadn't even been allowed to write a letter. She had no idea whether her mother had been able to bury the hatchet and telephone the man she despised so much, Hilde's father, Carl Dremmer, and his second wife, Emma.

Had Annie at least informed Q's mother, Ingrid?

The poor woman had turned seventy-six this year and had buried two of her sons and her husband already.

Worry about her children gnawed at Hilde's soul, eating her spirit bit by bit. Just when she wished she would die in this hellhole, a Gestapo officer came for her. Her neck hair stood on end as he pushed her upstairs into a room, equipped with a single chair and a table. Several minutes later, the door opened, and Hilde almost gasped at the sight of a neat and tidy woman.

"Here," the woman said and put a mug of water and an envelope on the table. Then she left without another word.

Hilde gulped down the cool, clear water before she reverently touched the envelope with her fingers, tracing the lines of Ingrid's old-fashioned handwriting. It took her several attempts to tear open the envelope with her trembling hands.

Dearest Hilde,

I have been in greatest sorrow since Frau Klein informed us about your and my son's arrest.

Every day I hope to hear that this was an unfortunate mistake and you and my Wilhelm have been released. Every day I have prayed that both of you will be able to spend Christmas at home with your children and me, the way we had planned.

If you are allowed to write, let me know how I can help, and if you need anything.

Frau Klein moved into your apartment in Nikolassee with the two boys, and she tried her best to care for them, but she also has to care for her sick husband. This is why she agreed to send Volker to your father in Hamburg. Unfortunately, my own health is declining rapidly, and I could not offer to care for my grandsons, even though you know how much I love them.

The letters blurred before Hilde's eyes, and she had to blink rapidly to clear them. Her two little boys. She missed them so much. She'd been very worried about Peter, with him being so little, but even more so about Volker. He was such a sensitive boy, and she could only imagine how this new situation was affecting him. And now to be separated from his brother.

He was usually excited to be with Grandma and Grandpa. Perhaps they could make him believe this was just a Christmas vacation? She wiped a tear away and continued to read.

Please rest assured, that both of your children are fine for the time being. My prayers and thoughts will always be with you.

Ingrid

Hilde sighed. She read the letter several times, and then folded it up and put it inside her bra, right over her heart. At least she had one connection to the outside world. Some time later, *Kriminalkommissar* Becker entered the room.

"*Frau* Quedlin, how are things at home? I understand you had a letter today?" Becker asked with a fake smile.

"Fine," she bit out, too raw to play his games. The letter had jumbled her emotions.

"That is excellent." Becker leered and took another step toward her. "It is unfortunate that such a beautiful woman like you married such a despicable bastard."

"Q is…" Hilde stopped. Why did she even care what Becker said? It was all part of his game.

He lifted an eyebrow. "Did you want to say anything?"

"No, sorry, *Kriminalkommissar*, I didn't want to interrupt you." Hilde steepled her hands, trying to steel herself for what was to come.

"Well, well. You are coming to your senses." His hand brushed her shoulders, and her entire body stiffened. "Your scumbucket of a husband has reaped what he sowed. The Reich will not let her enemies go unpunished, and he will pay the price for his treasonous acts. Execution. Doesn't that word melt on your tongue?"

If glaring daggers could kill, Becker would be dead by now.

"Execution. Say it. Say 'my scumbag traitor of a husband will be executed.'"

Bile rose in her throat as she repeated his words.

Becker showed a pleased smirk. "Well done, *Frau* Quedlin. I have the feeling you're beginning to cooperate. There is still a chance for you to save yourself, if you'd rather not follow in the footsteps of this *Drecksau*."

Hilde fought the urge to spit at him. *How dare he*!

"Tell me names. Every single person you suspect of having collaborated with the enemy. And you're free to leave."

Becker said it with an enticing smile, as if it was true, but Hilde only saw the hate, the cruelty, and the sadism in his eyes. The very things she'd suffered from in those past three weeks. Something snapped in her.

"I will tell you nothing! You have destroyed my life, taken me away from my children, beaten and abused me when I knew nothing about my husband's intelligence work. What makes you think I will believe you now? You...you...evil..." *bastard*.

As she thought the swear word, she instinctively ducked from the expected beating. But nothing happened. When Hilde looked up again, Becker was grinning from ear to ear, applauding her outburst.

"Are you done?" he asked, which only served to fuel the fire burning within her soul.

"No." She slammed her fist on the table, raising her voice, "I want to go home. I'm innocent. My children need me."

Kriminalkommissar Becker crossed his arms over his chest. "There is a way you can go home. Tell me what you know."

"I. Know. Nothing!" In her rage, she shoved the chair, knocking it over on its side. She paused as silence filled the room, sure this would have consequences.

Becker, though, seemed to be satisfied by witnessing her state of complete breakdown and ordered someone to take her back to her cell. There, she sank down onto the cold floor, pulled out the letter, and cried for a long time.

Chapter 10

For two long days, Q had been trying to come to terms with his death sentence. He'd assumed his life was forfeited the minute he'd been arrested. That assumption had now been confirmed in a secretive trial before a Nazi judge. And despite having expected the outcome, it still had hit him in the bowels. The look of agony on Hilde's face when he'd glanced into her eyes one last time.

Will I ever see her again? Or my sons?

Fear gripped him harder with every passing minute. It wasn't so much the fear of death because his rational brain understood it would be quick and rather painless. What had him in tight knots was what might come before that last breath.

Kriminalkommissar Becker had more than once stated how enraged Hitler himself was at Q's audacity to collaborate with the enemy *and* plan an assassination attempt on Goebbels. He'd never been shy with hints on *what else* his brutes had in store for uncooperative prisoners.

In the solitude of his death cell, Q's mind went down a dangerous path, envisioning and recalling the most appalling rumors he'd heard over the last years. Now that his trial was over, he'd never be shown in public again. What reason did the Gestapo have to keep him in one piece?

Terror took up every last cell in his body until he made a momentous decision. If he were going to die anyways, it would be on his own terms, by his own hand. Once he made the decision, he felt a peace and calm settle in his spirit. It would be his last act of defiance against this evil regime. With the prospect of agonizing torture, it was an easy, almost joyful task to plan his own demise.

The sun set and the guards had distributed what they called *food*. Q all but grinned at them, in the certainty that he'd never see their abhorred faces again. He waited until everything grew quiet beyond the doors of his cell. It was the perfect time. Nobody would make the rounds until morning.

He removed his glasses and broke them into pieces. Then he slipped beneath the wool blanket, the shards of glass clutched in his fingers. Q closed his eyes and thought of Hilde and his two little boys, and he almost lost his courage to go through with his plan. *Please forgive me.*

He pressed the shard of glass against his left wrist. The pain was slight, the rush of blood over his fingers warm and calming. After he slashed his right wrist, he waited for the inevitable to happen as he sensed his very life seeping into the mattress beneath him.

***

"Wilhelm Quedlin! *Aufstehen*! *Augen auf*!"

Q was floating on a cloud, looking down at the tiny city of Berlin, when a voice repeatedly insisted he open his eyes and stand up. He ignored the pesky voice, but it wouldn't shut up. Then hands grabbed his shoulders and shook him.

"*Er lebt*." He's alive.

How disappointing, Q thought and finally opened his eyes. Same cell. Same guards. Only this time, they were actually trying to save his life. *Stupid bastards. Let me die.* They wrapped his wrists with pieces of cloth, and fuzzy snippets of conversation reached his brain.

They pulled him from the mattress and attempted to get him to stand, but he'd lost too much blood, or not enough. He sank down to his knees, wavering like a tree in the storm.

"Take him to the hospital," someone said.

Q let everything happen to him like a puppet on a string, unable to move or talk. He was thrown onto a flat board and deposited in the back of an ambulance. A wave of nausea assailed him as the ambulance rushed off with the sirens wailing.

The drive to the prison hospital, Alt Moabit, didn't take long, and he was carried into the hospital ward. A stern-faced nurse and a physician examined his wounds and stitched the torn flesh of his wrists back together.

"Stupid man," the nurse said with a scowl. "You're lucky you didn't die."

Q's voice wouldn't work, or he would've told her how unlucky he was.

He was wheeled into a tiny cell with a large window in the center of the room, but he couldn't get up to look outside. As punishment for his attempt to take his own life, he was held in solitary confinement, wearing leather mittens, and tied to his bed so he wouldn't do something stupid again. The nurses fed him the minuscule half-rations, and for the rest of the day, he was alone with his thoughts. Nothing to occupy his mind. Nobody to talk to. No books to read. Nothing.

Q almost chuckled at the irony of fate. The same people who had sentenced him to death, wouldn't let him commit suicide. No, even his death had to be on their terms.

For most of the time, Q floated in a cloud of haze, trying to escape reality by solving mathematical puzzles, but not even his brain worked the way it was supposed to. The itching and burning wounds reminded him of his desolate situation, and the leather mittens over his hands made things worse.

The slashes didn't heal properly, and in the following days, the physician had to re-open the wounds twice to drain the infection from them. By the second day, copious amounts of suppuration soaked through his bandages. The young nurse gave him a wary smile before she exchanged his bandages. What she saw must have been awful because a look of horror crossed her face, and she hurried away to call the doctor.

After some consultation, they agreed to give Q penicillin.

"You shouldn't waste your precious penicillin on a man condemned to death," Q argued, but nobody took notice of him.

He slipped into a state of despondency, the infection, the constant hunger, and the boredom taking a toll on his body and soul. As he lay in his bed, hour upon hour, without books or any form of human interaction aside from the nurses twice a day, his mind began to unravel. It circled in a downward spiral.

Hilde.

His sons.

Gerald's betrayal.

His imminent death.

When will they come for me? How will I die? By firing squad? By guillotine?

Chapter 11

Hilde had finally been allowed to write a letter and was given one sheet of paper and a pen. She stared at the blank page for the longest time, thinking of her beloved family and wondering how Volker was adjusting to his new life with his grandparents in Hamburg.

Her father, Carl, had just turned fifty-seven years old, and she constantly worried about his health. Mother Emma… she smiled at the name. She had never called her stepmother "Mother" until Volker was born and Hilde became a mother herself. It was only then that she started to understand, and their relationship had improved.

She envisioned her half-sisters, twenty-one-year-old Julia and seventeen-year-old Sophie. Hilde wondered how much they had changed since she last saw them. There was so much she wanted to know. So much she wanted to say. But she was afraid of who else might read every word. Hilde sighed, and a tear fell as she began to write…

My dear mother and father,

Finally, I'm allowed to write. You were probably very scared when you received the news. I am fine, as far as you can be fine in my situation. Except for the horrific thoughts that follow me day and night.

Dad, please take my best wishes for your birthday, even though they come late. I wish you, from my deepest heart, love and all the best for the new year of your life, above all health. You know you are supposed to relax and not work so much.

Was Volker already with you for your birthday? You are now allowed to write me whenever you want. I believe you will be given the address you must write to. As you know, all letters will be read by the appropriate officials first.

I don't know anything about you and the children. Please write me about your lives. I miss you all so much. I only know that Volker is in Hamburg with you. I hope he is fine, at least I have wished so.

I hope he is not too much of a burden for you, dear Mother Emma, now that both of your daughters are also back to living with you. As long as Julia is not working, I hope she can help you, and the little boy gives you some pleasure and not only work.

We had been so looking forward to our first Christmas at home. The first time with our own Christmas tree, and also the first time with two children. How many Christmas holidays have we spent with you? Little Volker will think this celebration exists only at your place.

It consoles me that he will believe it is a good custom

and not some rupture in his life, and that he doesn't have to be somewhere with strange people and strange children.

Thankfully, Mother Annie agreed to take care of my sons when I was arrested, but I haven't seen or heard from her and have no idea how Peter is. There is so much I'd like to know. I was supposed to be allowed a visit from her a while ago, but nothing happened.

Was Julia in Berlin, and was it she who took Volker with her to Hamburg? I'm longing to know the details of his trip.

It was a true fortune, in my misfortune, that I finished sewing Volker's winter coat. I finished it on Friday, and Monday, November 30 was my unlucky day.

Hilde jumped when a guard yelled her name. She set down the pen and stood, her legs shaky beneath her. But he was only there to tell her she'd be transferred to a regular prison the next day.

"Pack your things and be ready," he yelled at her.

Which things? Hilde wanted to ask. She possessed nothing except the clothes she was wearing and the letter from Ingrid. She'd been wearing those same clothes nonstop since the day she'd been arrested more than three weeks ago, except for the two times she'd been stripped bare by her interrogators. Hilde stiffened at the memory.

It took several minutes until she was able to pick up her pen again. With a heavy heart, she continued to write...

When I finished the coat, I even told Q that if I were to die now, at least he had a memory of me, and that he would have to remind Volker that his mother loved him enough to spend many day and night hours making it especially for him.

I really said it as a joke. I had no idea what a horrible fate was already hovering over us.

But now, when he wears his winter coat, you can remind him of his mother. I hope he doesn't forget me and doesn't endure the same fate I did when I was his age. I still remember, as if it was yesterday, living with always changing relatives.

Not that they treated me badly, but I always knew that my mother didn't want me, and I longed to be back in my parental home. Knowing that the name of my mother was never mentioned, would be fearfully avoided, didn't make things better. Volker should know that I'm still here, and that I always think about him, and I hope deep in my soul that I will soon be together with him again.

If you have some, please show him pictures of me. Believe me, it will be solace for him even when he doesn't seem to be unhappy. Seeing pictures of his mother will help him remember me and keep our close relationship.

And he should not forget his little brother either. He shall know that he and Peter belong together always. Volker, despite his almost three years, is not a mindless kid *anymore, and I want that he will stay so thoughtful.*

We have always talked with him as if he was an adult, and his daddy has often said that he is a complete person. And now this complete person's life has changed a great deal. He had to give up those painting lessons with Auntie Stein, those he liked so much. Maybe you can write her a letter and have Volker paint something for her, she will be so happy.

He had to leave the Kindergarten where they just started with the advent celebrations and the Christmas carols and the other children of his age with whom he played so nicely. I'm sure he will also miss the nice little garden where he spent many hours a day outside.

I hope so much that all this he can have back very soon. Please do not misunderstand me, I know he is treated well by you, better than anywhere else except with me. And this is the reason why I want Volker to stay with you. Peter is, thank God, too small to comprehend all this. But it is even harder for me to leave him in this cute age.

All the joy he brought to my heart, every moment I spent with him. Oh God, it is so hard, but still not the hardest thing to do.

Hilde could not go on. Her shoulders shook too hard for her to continue writing. And even if she had been steady, she wouldn't have been able to see the paper through the blur of tears. She missed her children so badly. She was so afraid for them. For Q.

For herself.

Christmas was in two days, but save a miracle, she'd spend it in prison. Alone.

Amidst total darkness and desolation, she spotted the smallest silver lining. Tomorrow, she would leave the awful Gestapo headquarters behind and be transferred to a normal prison. A place without constant interrogations. A place where prisoners were treated like human beings. A place where she might be allowed clean clothes and a shower.

A shower! After three weeks in this hellhole, her clothes were covered in dried blood, dirt, and sweat. Mold and stench oozed from every pore.

Hilde curled up on the hard cot and fell into a nightmarish sleep. In that horrid place, it wouldn't take her mind long to slip into madness. It wasn't until morning that she felt steady enough to finish her letter.

You cannot imagine with how many tears I'm writing this letter. My first letter in this dreadful time of my life.

I can only write about my children because I have focused all my thoughts on them to help me in the darkest hours. Thinking of them warms my heart, but sometimes makes all of this so much more painful.

But I also know, and this has given me consolation, that with you and Dad, I will always have support. And that you will not be the only ones.

Now I must talk about the reason of my letter, the instructions on how to handle Volker. It is natural that he has to integrate into your way of life, but I must warn that he wakes up very early, around seven. If with you, he wakes up earlier, then he will have his nap time earlier as well and go to bed earlier in the evening.

My biggest wish in that regard is that he continues his naptime. He still needs it. At our house, he sleeps at least two hours and is still able to fall asleep immediately in the evening.

But he needs quiet and darkness when he is supposed to sleep, especially during the day. If he doesn't sleep, it's because he hasn't had enough exercise, especially outdoors.

My second wish is that he plays a lot outside, even if it rains. We have always played many hours outside, and I used to also let him play alone. It is my explicit wish, and he is used to doing so. Volker knows he's not supposed to step on the street. I have actually had to beat him two times because he did so. The second time, I hit him with a stick, the only time ever. He was seriously scolded and then spent half a day locked in a room.

But he had only followed other children; alone, he wouldn't have run onto the street. If he does the same thing at your place, I ask you to be as strict as I was because this is vitally important.

I grant my permission for you to give him a good smacking so he knows this is not just an empty threat when he doesn't do what you tell him. I'm sure it will work, but you have to be rigid and not grandmotherly.

Because now you must replace his strict mother.

I will ask Mother Annie to send you his hand cart to play outside as well as the sleigh he received last Christmas to keep him occupied. When it gets colder, he will need winter shoes because those from last year will not fit anymore. Mother Annie will have to apply for them.

I already applied for a pair of slippers for him. You should have received the ration coupon by now. All of this you will need to coordinate with Mother Annie. Give Volker gloves, scarf, etc. for playing outside.

I would love it if you could let him paint as often as he wants. Maybe you can help him with this. He loves painting.

Next, I must talk to you about nutrition. You know how badly sick Volker was and how long it took to recover from his stomach sickness. Therefore, please excuse me if I am very thorough about his nutrition because I do not want you to have the same problems with him again.

Hilde found great comfort in writing her son's daily requirements down, knowing this was the only motherly thing she could do for him right then. She guided Mother Emma on the foods he could eat and how often, letting her know what settled well on his stomach and what proved to upset it. When Volker turned three, he would get additional coupons for the extra nourishment the child needed. She hoped Emma and her father wouldn't be financially burdened by any of this.

Hilde racked her brain; trying to think of anything she had forgotten. She hated burdening Mother Emma with so many instructions, but what else could she do? She couldn't be a mother to her son right now, so all that was left was to mother as best as she could from afar.

When she was certain that she had covered everything, she rushed to finish the letter so it could be on its way to her beloved family...

I have a bad conscience about making you so many rules, I hope you don't think it's too much. May I ask you or Julia to please write me soon, letting me know in great detail how you all are? I'd like to know how Volker behaves, if he's healthy, if he is nice, what he does every day and how you spent Christmas, everything. I want to know everything.

Julia is such a good writer, please tell her to do this favor for her older sister.

Wishing you and my little sweetie a wonderful Christmas and a happy New Year. I'm sending greetings to everyone.

Your always thankful Hilde

She squeezed in some extra words on the sheet of paper she had been given.

My beloved little Volker,

Your mother had to write a letter because she couldn't come herself and this is why she's very sad.

But you spent Christmas with grandma and grandpa, this is fun, isn't it?

I hope you'll always be a good boy and do what grandma tells you. Maybe then there will be something nice under the Christmas tree, that lovely tree with so many lights.

Hilde stopped and drew a Christmas tree with candles and ornaments onto the paper.

I have painted a Christmas tree for you, can you do the same? Try it and then send it to your mother with a letter. Please don't forget your little brother, Peter, who is with your other grandma for Christmas.

But soon we will be all together again in our apartment in Nikolassee. Do you remember it? And then you can play again with your kindergarten friends.

Now, be always a good boy and please think once in a while about your mother who loves you more than anything in the world.

Hilde stared at the letter as tears rolled down her face once more. She folded the paper over, addressed the envelope, but didn't seal it. The censors would do that for her.

When the guard came for the letter, she was out of tears, despair crawling into every crevice of her being. Desperation was becoming her constant companion, and her ability to stay strong was slipping away with each passing hour.

Later in the morning, they came to transfer her to the women's prison. As soon as she left the Gestapo cellars behind, her spirit increased.

The new cell was about six by ten feet. It featured a bunk bed, a table, and a chair. Most importantly, there was a window where sunlight streamed inside.

Pure luxury.

Chapter 12

Christmas had passed, and the year 1943 had arrived when Q's wounds finally started to heal, and the constant mind-fog cleared. Two weeks tied to his bed in solitary confinement had made him hungry for any kind of human interaction.

As this wouldn't happen, he talked to himself aloud to break the monotony of his existence. He held vivid discussions with himself and was surprised when, one day a different voice filled the room.

He hadn't seen the young nurse before, or perhaps he just hadn't paid attention to her. She was little more than twenty years, with a round face, straight blonde hair, and vivid blue eyes.

"Are you feeling better, *Herr* Quedlin?" she asked him.

No, he definitely hadn't seen her before because nobody had ever addressed him by his name in this hospital. Usually, the nurses and doctors only barked orders at him. "*Hinsetzen. Essen. Aufstehen,*" Sit up. Eat. Stand.

"Well, yes," he managed to answer.

When she untied him and took off his mittens, he wasn't surprised. This had been the usual routine after the first few days. The nurses would untie him, give him his food, then sit in the corner, watching him while they read or wrote something.

Not this one. She helped him sit up, handed him the tray, and moved the chair to sit beside him.

"I'm *Schwester* Anna," she said.

Looking at her from nearby, she was much too thin. Like everyone in this country. While there wasn't a famine like during the Great War, the rations didn't allow anyone to put on fat.

"Thank you, I'm Wilhelm Quedlin," he said, out of training as to how to hold a conversation with another person besides himself.

She giggled. "I know that."

When he'd finished eating the piece of bread and two potatoes, she smiled at him and apologized. "I'm sorry, but I have to tie you up again."

Then she was gone. Q longed to see her again, but with her blonde hair and fair skin, she looked like an angel, and he came to the conclusion that she had been a trick of his isolated mind. A friendly *Krankenschwester* who actually talked to him? No way.

The next day she came back and started a conversation.

"You do know I've been sentenced to death,

Schwester Anna?" he asked her.

"Yes. We were told."

"Doesn't it strike you as ironic that you're nursing me back to health then?" Q rotated his wrists in all directions.

"It does, but that's my job." She paused for a while and lowered her voice. "You're luckier than your friends. Harro Schulze-Boysen, his wife, and another dozen members of the Red Orchestra were executed on December twenty-second."

"I knew he was arrested, but not that they'd already executed him," Q said. Apparently, *Schwester* Anna believed him to be part of Schulze-Boysen's network.

Another irony of fate. He and Schulze-Boysen had agreed not to work together, and yet he had been found out because they used the same contacts in Russia. According to what Q had heard in his trial and then put two and two together, the entire resistance network had been discovered when the Gestapo captured a female Russian parachutist last summer. She possessed a list of more than two hundred contacts, which the Gestapo had been able to decipher.

"The poor man, he'd been in Gestapo custody since last September. But he never wavered in his convictions," the nurse said.

Q's eyes widened in shock. Since September? How

come he hadn't known until his trial about Schulze-Boysen's arrest? Would he have been more careful? Stopped meeting Gerald? Would he still be free, together with his wife and sons?

Q barely noticed when *Schwester* Anna tied him to his bed again and left, too many emotions flooded his system. Guilt. Regret. Fear. He'd insisted on doing things on his own when he should have kept up with the news better.

After many hours of second guessing himself, analyzing all the possibilities, weighing the pros and cons, he finally found some calm. *There was nothing I could have done, and no way I could have known. I wouldn't have done a thing differently.*

When *Schwester* Anna returned in the morning, he'd been waiting for her, anxious to pepper her with questions. "Where did they shoot him?"

"He wasn't shot. He was hung," she said while untying Q.

"Hung?" Q raised an eyebrow. Military people like Schulze-Boysen were normally executed in front of a firing squad. Civilians were usually beheaded with the guillotine. *But hanging? Since when did the Nazis begin killing people by hanging them?*

Hanging was considered a discreditable and cruel method of execution. In a few rare situations, the drop broke the victim's neck, but more often than not, the rope merely compressed the throat, making breathing impossible and rendering the victim to a painful few minutes of suffering as they were suffocated to death. Their faces swelled and turned purple as the blood stopped its circulation, then blessedly, they would convulse and pass from this life.

"Yes. He made a statement before they dropped him." She turned her head away and whispered...

"Wenn wir auch sterben sollen,
So wissen wir: Die Saat
Geht auf. Wenn Köpfe rollen,
Dann Zwingt doch der Geist den Staat.
Glaubt mit mir an die gerechte Zeit, die alles reifen lässt!"

Even if we should die,
We know this: The seed
Bears fruit. If heads roll, then
The spirit nevertheless forces the state.
Believe with me in the just time that lets everything ripen.

Q didn't know what to say. Just reciting Schulze-Boysen's last words could get the nurse arrested if someone overheard her.

She turned to look at him with watery eyes. "So many brave men and women have been executed. Schulze-Boysen was so strong. He was brutally tortured, and yet he never said a word or betrayed anyone working with the Resistance. He didn't even beg for his life."

"You shouldn't voice these things here. People

have been arrested for less," Q warned her.

A smile appeared on her face. "Would you turn me in?"

"Of course not. But the walls have ears. You never know who's listening, or whom to trust," he said, tasting the bitterness of Gerald's betrayal.

In this moment, the door opened, and the head nurse peeked inside. She scowled at Anna. "Hurry up, you are needed. And have I heard chatter in here?"

"Yes, *Oberschwester*, I just told the prisoner to finish his meal so I can leave. I'll be with you in a minute," *Schwester* Anna answered.

The next day, another nurse attended him.

When she left, it finally dawned on him, what his sentence actually meant. Death.

Of course, he had known the meaning on an intellectual level, but now, he felt the weight of it in every cell. His body took on a life of its own and started shaking violently, and for once, he was thankful to be tied to his bed. After hours of howling, screaming, and fighting, he finally fell asleep.

When he woke up the next morning, he consoled himself with the fact that at least Martin would continue their sabotage work at Loewe, even without Erhard and Q. In case of an upheaval from within Germany, Martin would also be able to lead the company into a new era.

Chapter 13

The deafening sound of air raid alarms penetrated Hilde's dreams on January sixteenth. The next moment she was wide awake. It was her first alarm in prison. She heard the guards rushing along the hallway and waited for someone to open her cell door. But nothing happened.

Her cellmate, a resolute Polish woman in her fifties with little mastery of the German language, said, "Prisoners stay in cells."

Hilde looked at her in shock. That couldn't be true. Their cell was on the third floor, and they were sitting ducks to the British bombers.

"No, no," Hilde protested. "We need to go to the shelter. Or at least to the basement of the building."

"Yes. Stay," the woman said and stretched out on her cot, sliding a rosary through her fingers and murmuring a verse in Polish that Hilde assumed to be *Hail Mary*.

Not sure whether the protection of the Virgin Mary would extend to a protestant, Hilde wrapped a blanket around her slight form and cowered in the corner of the cell. The building shook as bomb after bomb detonated nearby. Dust and pieces of the plaster walls fell to the floor, and she coughed in the dusty air.

The air raid continued for most of the night and finally stopped sometime after the sun came up. Covered with dust, Hilde climbed the ladder to her bunk bed, eyeing the peacefully sleeping Polish woman with envy before she fell into a fitful sleep.

A few days after the bombing, the guard announced a visitor for Hilde. It would be the first person from outside she'd seen since her arrest almost two months ago.

Hilde entered the visiting room to find a man she hadn't seen before.

"*Frau* Quedlin, my name is Müller, and I'm your lawyer." He extended his hand to her.

Hilde took it, baffled. "My lawyer? But–"

"*Frau* Klein has retained me to defend you and your husband."

"My mother?" Hilde asked, confused by his words.

"Yes, your mother, Annie Klein, has hired me to mount a defense against the Gestapo's accusations."

Hilde couldn't believe it. It wasn't at all like her mother. The same person who hadn't even written a letter had gone to all the trouble to hire a costly lawyer to defend her?

"Please tell her that I'm very grateful, but I

can't..."

The lawyer waved her objection away and pulled a sheaf of papers from his briefcase. "Let's sit down and get over the paperwork first. Shall we?"

Hilde took a seat and eyed the papers.

Herr Müller explained about his duties and his fees, then slid the first document across to her and handed her a pen. "This is a full power over your and your husband's estate for your mother. According to the contract, she has to use it in good faith to cover all expenses related to your children and to pay my fees."

Hilde shook her head, her earlier surprise replaced by the bitter knowledge of her mother's ulterior motives. Annie never did anything if there wasn't an advantage to her.

"I know this may seem like picking over bones, but it actually is the best solution. Your mother, *Frau* Klein, has the best intentions."

Yes, the best intentions for herself.

After a long pause, *Herr* Müller tapped the paper. "Your trial is scheduled in less than a week."

"I will sign it, fine, but you need to get my husband's signature as well," Hilde said and reluctantly took the pen.

"Of course I will, *Frau* Quedlin. As soon as I'm allowed to visit him."

The lawyer asked her about her side of the story,

and she repeated everything she'd already told the Gestapo. He might be her lawyer, but she was sure someone was watching or listening, so she made sure that she didn't confess to having done anything illegal. Nor would she ever mention Martin's name. As far as she knew, he was still in liberty.

"Very good. That should help." *Herr* Müller finished scribbling notes and looked at her with a sad expression in his eyes. "You have been accused of high treason."

"High treason?" Hilde's voice quivered.

"Unfortunately, yes."

"This is ridiculous. I've done nothing to justify..." Her voice broke, and she took a deep breath.

"That is what we need to prove at trial."

"But...how can they...?" Hilde closed her eyes and willed her voice to work. "What are my chances?"

"This I don't know. I promise I'll do my best, but I will be honest with you. Your trial is considered *Geheime Kommandosache*."

"What does that mean?" Hilde wanted to know.

"It means the normal sharing of information is suppressed. I asked for copies of the evidence against you but have received nothing. We won't see the evidence they intend to use until the day of the trial."

"But that's unlawful!" Hilde was livid. She stood up and paced the small room. "How can they do this? There are laws in place for a reason."

"Laws they do not have to follow."

Desperation gripped her. "Is there nothing that can be done?"

"I am going to do my best for you. Furthermore, I've started the paperwork to appeal Q's sentence. I won't be able to overturn his conviction, but I'm hoping to get his sentence changed to lifelong imprisonment instead of execution." With a glance at his watch, *Herr* Müller stuffed his papers back in his briefcase and stood up. "My time is up, but I will be back. Have a good day, *Frau* Quedlin."

A good day?

Chapter 14

Q was lying on his bed, trying to exercise his weakened and sore body within the little free moving space he had when the door to his cell opened. Judging by the sun streaming in through the window, it was around noon. A very unusual time for anyone to enter his room.

At the sight of the head nurse, his heart sank, but she greeted him with something similar to a smile.

"*Herr* Quedlin, you have a visitor." She released his hands and feet and helped him sit on the edge of the bed before ushering in a thin, well-dressed man a few moments later.

"Doctor Quedlin, allow me to introduce myself. I am *Rechtsanwalt* Müller, and I am here to represent you," the lawyer said and extended his hand.

"Who sent you?" asked Q, suspicious of being allowed a visitor after all these weeks.

"Your mother-in-law, Annie Klein, has retained me to represent you and your wife against the charge presented and your conviction."

Q nodded, trying to grab hold of what the man was saying. "Have you seen my wife?"

"Yes, I have. She sent me to tell you she's fine and looking forward to her trial with hope, as she's innocent."

Q smiled at the evidence that Hilde stuck to their plan to lay all guilt on him and pretend to be an unknowing helper.

"Do you know when her trial will be?" he asked.

"As a matter of fact, in three days from now. But I'm here to talk about your case, not hers, if you understand." *Herr* Müller glanced at his watch. "We have only twenty-five minutes left."

Q raised a bandaged hand. "Excuse me, but first, why now? Why is the Gestapo allowing this?"

"Well, it is my understanding that *Frau* Klein is well connected. She personally asked *Kriminalkommissar* Becker for this favor, and it was granted to her."

A favor? Since when is being allowed a lawyer to defend yourself a favor? Q wanted to scream but refrained from doing so. It wouldn't help. He'd be grateful for this *favor* that actually was a basic right – or had been before Hitler came to power.

Herr Müller pulled some papers from his briefcase and handed them to Q with a pen. "These papers transfer all legal power over your estate to your mother-in-law so that she may continue to care for your children and pay my fees. I need you to sign on the line next to where your wife signed."

Q's thankfulness disappeared. He wasn't at all surprised that Annie had figured out a way to benefit from his and her daughter's arrests. His first impulse was to refuse, but his children needed food and clothing and a place to live. All of this cost money. Sure, he had given his mother an envelope with money to stash away, but this money wouldn't last for long if it was the only source of income for his children.

"I knew there was a catch," he sighed in disgust as he signed his name. It rankled that he was forced to transfer all of his property and wealth to his mother-in-law. Even if it was for his own defense and the good of his children.

Herr Müller proceeded to talk about his plans to appeal Q's sentence and turn it into lifelong prison instead of a death sentence.

As long as *lifelong* meant the duration of Hitler's Third Reich and not Q's life, Q didn't mind. He was convinced that the "Thousand Year Empire" wouldn't last but another year or two at most.

At the end of their half-hour discussion, the lawyer tucked the papers away. "I've also contacted Ingrid Quedlin and Gunther Quedlin."

"You've talked with my mother and brother?" Q asked, perplexed.

"Yes. Your brother has kindly offered to help as much as is needed," *Herr* Müller said while getting ready to leave.

"Please give my best wishes and my thanks to him," Q said hesitantly. Gunther was a lawyer himself, but Q wasn't sure how he felt about dragging his brother into this mess. He'd had enough grief in his own life, having been forced to retire from his job at the Ministry of Education shortly after the Nazis came into power due to being a member of the social democratic party.

"There appears to be some tension between *Frau* Klein and your side of the family."

Q chuckled, the first one in a long time. "More than you imagine. My mother hates *Frau* Klein. Gunther hates Hilde and *Frau* Klein. *Frau* Klein hates her ex-husband, who is Hilde's father. She also hates his second wife. Hilde hates her mother. And believe it or not, even my mother and brother have been hot and cold for as long as I can remember. In this family, nobody talks with anybody and grudges are held onto for life."

The attorney chuckled and shook his head. "It's really a shame when families cannot get along with one another. Really a shame. Have a good day." *Herr* Müller shook Q's hand, then knocked on the door to be let outside.

As they waited for the door to open, the lawyer turned to look at Q and said, "Propaganda minister Goebbels has called for total war. He's supposed to hold a speech in Sportpalast."

Q paled. Goebbels' *total war* was one that had been

rumored as a last resort. The Reich would be closing down and monitoring all civilian activities. Anything that didn't directly help the war effort would be shut down, and the people put to work elsewhere. No one, not even the rich, would be able to escape the demands of the Party.

He also knew that if it had come to this, the war would continue mercilessly until one of the parties surrendered unconditionally. And it wouldn't be the Allies. The hardships the German people had suffered were only just beginning.

Chapter 15

January 27, 1943

Hilde looked into the heavily spotted mirror and braided her hair as best as she could. The day of her trial had arrived, and she wanted to look like a good, and innocent, German housewife.

Everyone, including her lawyer and the prison guards, had told her that, in the worst case, she'd be sentenced to five to ten years in jail. The most probable outcome was one to two years, and with some luck, she'd be allowed to go home today.

Normally, prisoners were allowed to take a shower once a week, in groups of ten. Ten women. Three showers. Twenty minutes. Still it was a luxury compared to the Gestapo cellars.

But today, she'd been given twenty minutes alone in the showers in order to look nice for her trial. It was a special concession given by *Frau* Herrmann. She was in her early twenties, and her wavy blonde hair fell down on her shoulders, giving her an angelical look. But that wasn't the reason the women called her *Blonde Angel*.

They had given her the nickname because she was

always helping the prisoners in one way or another. She smuggled secret messages in and out, never withheld news from the outside, snuck them extra rations or other small favors when possible, and always had a nice word and smile on her lips – for everyone. She truly was an angel.

Hilde smiled. She'd learned to find joy in the smallest things, like taking an extra shower.

Her fingers trembled as she finished braiding her long brown hair. She'd spent the time since her lawyer announced the date of her trial vacillating between hope and despair. He hadn't visited again, nor had anyone else. Not even *Kriminalkommissar* Becker and his henchmen.

Not that she missed them, but it had left her with way too much time on her hands to think. About the past. About Q. About her two little boys. About her mother and the future…it was an emotional ride.

"You look nice," *Fräulein* Hermann said, "the automobile is waiting for you."

My automobile is waiting for me? Hilde suppressed a giggle but nonetheless felt a tiny bit like royalty.

Frau Herrmann escorted her down and handed her over to two male police officers. "Good luck."

The police weren't unfriendly and helped her get into the back of the truck. Apparently, normal police still had some manners.

The truck stopped, the door opened, and another

prisoner climbed inside. His nose had been broken, and green and black bruises disfigured his face. It took Hilde a few moments to recognize the newcomer.

"Hello, Erhard," she said.

He blinked and looked at her with a dull expression on his face. His eyes probably had to adapt to the darkness in the truck first.

A police officer jumped inside and shackled Erhard to the wall opposite her.

"Hello, Hilde," Erhard greeted her, his voice thick.

"No talking," the policeman ordered and jumped out. Hilde heard him bolt the door, and a few seconds later, the vehicle started moving again.

With barely audible whispers, she talked to Erhard. His wife had also been arrested, but they'd released her after a few days.

Hilde decided to take it as a good omen.

The truck stopped in front of the courthouse, and she and Erhard were escorted up the steps and seated together on the defendant's bench. Despite not being allowed to speak to one another, his mere presence gave her strength.

Hilde skimmed the room for her lawyer. She thought he would be seated beside her, but she finally found him sitting next to *Kriminalkommissar* Becker on the side of the prosecutor. Her stomach sank.

To her right was the judge's bench, and to her left, the audience. Most people in the audience wore a uniform, except for one man with curly blond hair.

Her heart leaped as she sought his eyes. Q looked miserable. Thin and weak, the fire in his curious blue eyes had dimmed. She sent him a smile and hoped he could see in her eyes how much she loved him.

The trial began. Erhard's case was first. He'd confessed to being a tacit accomplice, hoping to receive a jail sentence.

After a pause of several minutes, where she leaned her shoulder against Erhard's to give him some comfort, the trial continued with her case.

Herr Müller argued for her innocence. "Your honor, *Frau* Quedlin is a housewife and mother. She has given the *Führer* two beautiful sons. She didn't understand what she was typing for her husband. Furthermore, she had no active role in the sabotage at the Loewe radio factory."

Kriminalkommissar Becker argued the charges against her and stepped forward. "How does a woman, living in such harmony with her husband for seven years, not know he's a traitor to the Reich? I tell you, she knew what she was typing and even encouraged his criminal sabotage activities."

"I do not see any evidence to convince me she was not complicit with the espionage and sabotage taking place," the judge agreed with Becker.

"This woman deserves to pay the ultimate price for her part in defying the Party, the *Führer*, and the Reich," *Kriminalkommissar* Becker demanded.

Herr Müller argued the exact opposite fiercely, "Your honor, this woman doesn't deserve to die for her unknowing actions. Even if you deem her guilty – and I believe she isn't – of complicity, according to paragraph..."

Hilde didn't understand most of the legal gibberish, except that her actions were of such minor importance to the operation that she should be punished with a prison sentence of no more than two years.

Hope settled in her heart. She gathered all of her strength and energy around her, showing a mask of airiness to the cold and contemptuous Nazi supporters in the courtroom. On the inside, however, she was worried not only for her own life but also for the well-being of her two little boys.

When some official looking person announced a recess and Hilde was taken outside, dread boiled in her belly as something became clear...

These Nazi devils were on a roll to kill anyone who opposed them. Was it Erhard's and her turn now?

Chapter 16

Q sat in the courtroom, well aware of the importance of this day for the fates of his family. Even the most die-hard Nazi supporters in the audience seemed to agree that while Erhard deserved the death sentence, Hilde should get away with a few years in prison.

The shy smile on her thinned face and the carefully braided hair in Pretzel-style surely had helped to win the sympathy of the judge, too.

When Q was told to get up and leave the courtroom to await the judge's decision, his weak legs barely held his body weight, and he had to lean on the bench to stand. He moved slowly towards the exit, his stomach growling in protest.

In the prison hospital, he'd received only half rations. Half of the smaller prisoner rations, not the ones for civilians. After just two months in custody, his clothes bagged on him, and it was only thanks to the suspenders that he didn't lose his pants.

He was afraid of what the judge would decide but chose to stick with hope. His friend had been incredibly brave and steadfast during the trial. An example of courage in the face of terrible odds. Not once had Erhard cried, whined, or begged. But civil courage and honesty weren't traits honored by this regime.

And Hilde...if she wasn't already the woman of his dreams, he would have fallen in love with her today. Even when *Kriminalkommissar* Becker had demanded the capital punishment, she hadn't even flinched.

The guard cuffed Q's left hand to the bench in the waiting area and left. A few moments later, another guard showed up with Hilde in tow. He cuffed her to the same bench.

Q's heart lurched. Suddenly, the room seemed to beam with sunlight.

"The judge will have lunch and render his verdict in one hour," the guard said and disappeared.

Q looked at his beautiful wife and reached for her arm with his free hand. Her skin was so soft, but her eyes widened in horror. Q followed her glance down to the bulging scar on his wrist.

"What happened?" she whispered.

Q felt his face flush, but he met her eyes. "After my sentencing, I decided I would rather take my own life than allow these devils to take it from me. But I failed."

"Oh, *Liebling*! What did they do to you?" Hilde asked, lifting his wrist, and kissing the scar softly.

"They moved me to the prison hospital, and I've

been there ever since." He didn't tell her about being kept in solitary confinement or the fact that he'd been tied to his bed most of the time.

"I've missed you so much," Hilde said with tears in her eyes.

"My love. I've thought endlessly about you and our boys."

Hilde nodded, and her tears spilled over. "Will we ever see them again?"

Q lifted his hand and cupped her jaw, searching her eyes, wishing there was some way he could make this all go away for her. "They are being cared for, and that is what counts right now."

Hilde nodded and laid her head on his shoulder, their hands intertwined. Q kissed her forehead, then sat with her, closing his eyes and soaking up this moment. This one hour might be all the time in this life he'd be allowed to spend with her, and he vowed to keep these memories deep inside his soul. For eternity.

"Remember when we first met?" he asked her, not really expecting an answer. "You were so beautiful and full of life. Your laughter in the movies had me intrigued even before I'd seen you. I knew then that you were the woman for me."

Hilde turned her head and looked up at him. "We've had a good life together, haven't we?"

"Yes. And no matter what happens, know that I

love you with all of my heart and soul."

"I love you, too." She stopped speaking and leaned as close to him as her handcuff allowed. The warmth of Hilde leaning against him seeped into his soul, mind, and body.

They stayed like that, remembering the good times. They laughed, giggled, and cried. They packed their entire life together into this time.

She was his soulmate and would always be. In this life or the next.

Far too soon, the guards returned and took them back into the courtroom for the proclamation of the sentences.

The judge entered the courtroom and instructed Erhard to stand. The tension was palpable, and Q's neck hair stood on end.

"Doctor Erhard Tohmfor, it is the ruling of this court that you are found guilty on all counts and are hereby sentenced to death by execution."

The audience applauded. Erhard's face showed the shock for a short moment before he gathered his composure and stared defiantly at the judge.

Q sent his friend a short nod in acknowledgment of his courage.

"*Frau* Quedlin, please stand."

Hilde squared her shoulders and stood erect and tall, despite the fact that she must be scared to death.

Q wished with everything in him that he could be there to hold her hand in this moment. He closed his eyes, listening for the words that would spare her life.

"*Frau* Quedlin, I have looked at the evidence that has been presented to this court. I find it incredible that a woman so in love with her husband would not be aware of his subversive activities. I, therefore, find you guilty of cognizance of high treason and sentence you to death by execution."

Q's eyes popped open. *Sentenced to death? Not prison? God, no! That cannot be true.*

But it was. Hilde's gasp of dismay could be heard among the murmurs in the audience. Apart from the gasp, she stood upright and unwavering, defying everything the judge stood for.

Judging by the puzzled then smug look crossing *Kriminalkommissar* Becker's face, not even the Gestapo had expected such a harsh verdict.

The judge slammed his gavel down on the bench and left the courtroom.

Q's mind remained in in a fog as he tried to process what just happened. He barely noticed the guard leading him to the waiting vehicle outside, murmuring something that sounded like *Sorry*.

When Q's eyes had accustomed to the darkness inside, he couldn't believe what he saw. Hilde.

Q looked at the prison guards and silently

thanked them for their compassion. There seemed to be a good heart buried beneath their harsh appearances. The door was bolted from the outside. He and Hilde were alone.

He flung her into his arms. He touched her beautiful face, scrutinized it, trying to memorize every single line, the sweetness, her bright blue eyes, her red and soft lips.

He kissed those lips. Careful at first, but soon, red-hot fire passed between them. They both knew this would be their last kiss. They wrapped their arms around each other and hungrily devoured the other's mouth.

When they had to come up for air, they whispered words of love, but also cautioned each other to be strong.

He locked eyes with Hilde and felt the fire in his body ignite. The fire that had been burning between them from the first moment he saw her and that had never ceased to burn during all those years. Not even now, when they both were sentenced to death.

"I love you," she whispered.

"I'm so sorry, darling." Q kissed her neck, intent on memorizing the feel of his wife in his arms.

"It wasn't your fault. Don't you ever blame yourself for this awfulness." She looked at him, sad, but steadfast in her conviction.

A rock fell from his shoulders. Not even after her

harsh sentence did she blame him. Much too soon the door of the truck was opened, and one of the guards peeked inside. "We have to leave."

Q nodded and said to Hilde one last time, "I love you." Then he was hurried away and could only wave to the disappearing car.

Chapter 17

For days after the trial, Hilde refused to talk to anyone. Her cellmate, the Polish woman, had been transferred to some other place, and she was alone in her cell.

The other women on her level had soon decided to let Hilde grieve and didn't insist on making conversation. Everyone understood that a death sentence was hard to swallow.

On the third day, the Blonde Angel appeared with a pretty young woman and introduced her as Hilde's new cellmate Margit Staufer.

Hilde did her best to ignore the woman. Although girl would be more correct. She couldn't be much older than eighteen. But seeing the newcomer so lost and sad tugged at her motherly feelings, and she couldn't keep to herself any longer.

"I apologize for my earlier rudeness. I'm Hilde. Welcome to this humble place." She made a gesture showing the entire cell.

For a short moment, the girl's face lit up. "Thank you. I'm Margit."

"You look so young," Hilde said, wondering what

she could have done to end up here.

"I turned nineteen three months ago." Margit bit her fingernails and looked hesitantly at Hilde. "How long have you been here?"

"I was arrested two months ago."

Margit's eyes widened. "That long?"

Hilde nodded, not mentioning her death sentence. The two women talked about their lives, and soon became friends.

Two days later, Margit received a huge package.

Hilde watched as Margit opened the large box and unpacked more food than Hilde had seen in a long time. Her stomach rumbled at the smell of smoked ham. The minuscule prison rations were enough not to starve, but it never left her sated.

Margit generously shared the food with Hilde and waved away her weak protest.

"If I want more, my family will send me more. Please eat."

"Thank you." Hilde took tiny pieces of ham, fresh bread, apples, and even a morsel of cake. It was the first time in months that she didn't feel the constant nagging of hunger.

After a while, Margit asked, "So, what did you do?"

Hilde looked at Margit, trying to gauge if she really was who she pretended to be. It wasn't unusual to plant spies in prisons to get information the regime wouldn't otherwise find out. But Hilde was already convicted, so what difference did it make?

"My husband has relayed intelligence to our enemies, and I was accused of helping him."

Margit scowled. "These Nazis…they are an insult to true Germans everywhere."

"Shush! Aren't you afraid someone will hear you?" Hilde urged her.

"I will not be silenced." Margit threw her head back.

Hilde smiled. Margit was the spitting image of herself – a decade ago when she'd been young and hot-blooded. Determined to right the injustices around her. Before she'd grown up and stopped voicing her concerns openly, afraid of the consequences.

And what has that served you? Nothing! Absolutely nothing!

Looking back on her life now, she wished she'd done more. Taken a more active role in the Resistance efforts instead of just supporting Q's work. But she'd had children to take care of…still, a pang of jealousy hit her as she witnessed Margit's carefreeness. That girl simply refused to succumb to the necessities of life or let the Nazis threaten her.

Over the next days, Hilde and Margit became

friends. Hilde enjoyed their conversations and the point of view of a teenager. In Margit's life, everything was still easy. Black and white.

Having someone to talk to relieved the boredom and helped keep her mind busy. It was only when she lay down to sleep, and the cell grew quiet that her mind rolled back to Q, her little boys, and the death sentence that loomed over her head.

Chapter 18

After Hilde's trial, Q was told he'd be transferred to the Plötzensee prison. His initial thrill of leaving the solitary confinement of the Moabit prison hospital was crushed when *Kriminalkommissar* Becker walked into his hospital cell with a satisfied grin.

"Prisoner. You couldn't wait to be dead, could you? But let me tell you that I'm the one to decide when and how it happens, not you. And I might just let you rot in prison for a while, wouldn't that be fun?"

Q chose not to take the bait. "*Herr Kriminalkommissar*, what a surprise to see you here."

"I happened to be in the area and thought I would let you know that your mother has requested permission to visit you."

"My mother?" Hope flared in Q. Usually, prisoners had the right to receive visitors once per month, and his old mother had gone to the trouble to visit Becker in the Gestapo Headquarters across the city from her place to receive a visiting permit.

"I denied it," Becker stated.

Q felt his spirit deflate. So much for seeing his

mother one last time. He swallowed down his angry retort and asked, "May I ask why?"

"You have shown so little cooperation, I decided you didn't deserve the privilege of visitors," Becker said with a cruel smile.

Since when had yet another lawful right become a *privilege?* Hatred for the Gestapo officer choked Q, and it was all he could do to hold his tongue and keep from verbally attacking the horrid man. He slumped down on his bed and stared at the floor.

"I hope you enjoy your new cell as much as you enjoyed our hospitality at Prinz-Albrecht-Strasse," Becker said and left.

This one sentence brought memories to the surface that Q had carefully buried deep down for the past month. Angst seeped into every single bone, and his entire body trembled violently.

When the nurse entered the room a few minutes later, she knew with one glance on his face what had happened and muttered under her breath, "I really don't know why we coddle the patients, and then give them back to the Gestapo."

She helped him get up and turned him over to the prison guards who'd just arrived.

At Plötzensee, the guards shoved him into a cell that actually looked like a place where someone could live. The nine by twelve feet space held a chair, a table, a closet, and a bunk bed. The bed was completely equipped with a mattress and a rough woolen blanket. Compared to the Gestapo cellar, this was luxury.

Q sat on the lower bed and jumped when a voice from above said, "Hello, my name is Werner Krauss." A head with slightly too long, dark hair popped over the side and looked down at him from the upper bed.

"I'm Wilhelm Quedlin, but friends call me Q."

"Q it is then. I believe we'll have to keep each other company, whether we like it or not." Werner climbed down from the upper bed and extended his hand.

Q immediately liked the dry humor of his cellmate. Judging by the way he talked, the man must be educated.

"Well, I would say it's nice to meet you, but I think we both agree it would have been better to never meet than to meet here," Q said as he shook the extended hand.

Werner answered with a dry laugh. "I was getting crazy, talking only to myself."

Over the next days, Q learned that Werner Krauss was indeed educated. He'd been a professor of literary sciences in Marburg before he was conscripted to the Wehrmacht and then transferred to Berlin. Q already looked forward to many fruitful arguments with his new cellmate. At least something was positive in his otherwise bleak life.

At one point, Q asked Werner about the bright red pieces of cloth tied to the bars of some of the prison cells, including theirs.

"TU. *Todesurteil*," Werner said with a crooked smile. "So everyone knows the inmates have been sentenced to death."

"Ah. You too." Q swallowed and finally dared to ask the question he'd been avoiding all these days. "How does a professor end up on death row?"

"A very good question," Werner agreed. "Via one of my friends, I made the acquaintance of Harro Schulze-Boysen. One thing came to another, and I ended up helping his group put up posters against the exposition *The Soviet Paradise*."

"You mean the propaganda exposition they did last year in June? The one full of lies about the Soviet Union? Showing how people live in earth holes?"

"That one," Werner answered.

"And you received a death sentence for pasting posters?" Q shook his head. He'd known that, according to the *Volksschädlingsverordnung*, the decree about damages to the nation, every criminal act could be avenged with the capital penalty. But gluing posters?

"That, and listening to foreign radio transmissions."

Q chuckled.

"What's so funny?" Werner asked him.

"It's just that I bought a *Volksempfänger* back in 1935 and adapted it to receive foreign radio stations. But that is the one thing the Gestapo never found out."

Werner grinned. "I won't tell them."

Werner had influential friends in the intellectual community and had secret channels to receive real news, not the Goebbels propaganda. One day in early February, he received a visitor and came back to their cell with exciting news.

"Q. We have a reason to celebrate."

"Your appeal was granted," Q asked warily. It wasn't that he begrudged his friend, but he would miss his company.

"No. That will come." Werner waved it away. "Have you heard what is going on outside these walls?"

Q shook his head.

"My visitor just told me that a few days ago, the *Wehrmacht* had to surrender at Stalingrad."

"Wow. You sure this is true? It would be the first blow to Hitler's confidence in this war."

"It is true. Hitler refused to speak on the tenth anniversary of his coming to power and Goebbels had to give the speech for him. And, hold your breath, Goebbels has ordered to close down all theaters, movies, varietées, and other entertainment establishments until February 6 to commemorate the devastating defeat of the *Wehrmacht*."

Q and Werner discussed for endless hours the possible implications to the Eastern front, the Western front, the public mood in Germany and in the occupied countries. They also discussed Goebbels *total war* declaration and what that might mean for the citizens of Germany. They discussed the Resistance effort and how they hoped the Russian's would continue to push back the Nazi army.

Despite the distraction Werner provided, Q was riddled with guilt. Hilde had forgiven him, but he couldn't do the same. It was his fault that she'd been sentenced to death, and there was nothing in the world that could take this burden from his shoulders.

Chapter 19

Three long weeks had passed since Hilde's trial when the Blonde Angel opened her cell.

"You have a visitor," *Frau* Herrmann said.

"A visitor?" Hilde beamed with joy. A visitor was something all prisoners longed for, and for her, it was the first time other than her attorney.

Frau Herrmann took her to the visiting room and said, "I'll be back in one hour. Enjoy."

Hilde gave her a grateful smile and entered the room where Annie was waiting for her.

"Mother?" Hilde walked the short distance to her mother, and then stopped dead in her tracks, incapable of believing her own eyes.

"What's wrong, dear," Annie asked. "You look like you've seen a ghost?"

"I am. You are wearing my coat." Hilde wanted to slap her mother in the face for appropriating the fur coat that Q had given her for Christmas when she was pregnant with Volker.

Annie tossed her head and rolled her eyes. "Well, it's not like you were using it, and it's such a nice coat. Besides, it's been freezing for weeks, and you wouldn't want me to catch a chill."

"You could have at least asked. I'm not dead yet, you know?" Hilde longed to rip the coat off her mother.

"Of course you're not dead, my dear, or I wouldn't be visiting, would I? Hilde, let me have a look at you." Annie had the annoying habit not to reply to anything she didn't like.

Hilde sighed. Maybe her mother should have the fur coat; she wouldn't be allowed to keep it in prison anyways.

"You look good. But you should really eat more, you're too thin."

"Mother..." Hilde groaned inwardly. Had her mother no idea about reduced rations and those formalities? "How did you get permission to visit me?"

"Oh darling, it wasn't hard. Sit with me." Annie patted the chair beside her. "All I had to do is ask *Kriminalkommissar* Becker for permission. We had a wonderful chat, and he encouraged me to personally ask him whenever I want to visit. Within reason of course. He's such a lovely man and so handsome in his Gestapo uniform."

Hilde rolled her eyes. Her mother would be the only person in the world to use the words *Gestapo* and *lovely* in the same sentence.

"Trust me, there is nothing *lovely* about him,"

Hilde protested.

"That's because you don't want to see things as they are. I'm sure if you had decided to stay within the law, you two would get along so well. He's the dream of every mother-in-law. Polite, upright, firm in his opinions. Loyal to our *Führer*."

"He's a monster," Hilde hissed, and her entire body tensed with the memory of the interrogations in the Gestapo headquarters. If her mother knew Becker's true colors, she'd stop gushing about him. But Hilde wouldn't enlighten her; those dark hours were something she wanted to keep locked deep inside, never to surface again.

"Your husband is the monster." Annie shook her head. "You know none of this would have happened if you'd married a man like *Kriminalkommissar* Becker and not that dishonorable husband of yours. I will never forgive myself for not seeing through him earlier and even allowing you to marry him."

"I don't remember asking for your permission," Hilde quipped.

"Well, that is your problem. You don't ask your mother. You always were a difficult girl, out causing trouble and disobeying the authorities. I'm not surprised you ended up here. I should have drowned you in the first bath water."

Hilde took a deep breath. She'd heard that insult so many times, she shouldn't care anymore. "Mother, it's not his fault. He has loved me like no other man ever could. I don't blame him and will continue to love him until I take my dying breath."

"See how his love has ruined your life! You don't have to die for him." Annie dabbed at her eyes.

"Mother, please." Hilde didn't want to fight with her mother. "Tell me about the boys."

Annie leaned back with a theatrical sigh. "Berlin wasn't a good place for them. I had to send both of them to your father in Hamburg. His new wife has more time on her hands than I do."

"I'm sure Emma will take good care of them." Hilde tried to keep a straight face as she nodded. It hadn't taken Annie long to figure out that raising children was a lot of work and interfered with her busy social schedule. Deep inside her heart, Hilde was relieved to know her sons were in the capable hands of her stepmother.

"Thank you for helping out, Mother. And for contacting the lawyer."

Annie beamed with pride. "No big deal. By the way, I almost forgot. I brought food and money." She handed Hilde a package wrapped in plain brown paper.

Hilde unpacked black bread, cheese, ham, and precious sugar along with several bank notes.

"*Kriminalkommissar* Becker told me you can use the money to send extra letters if you wish. Because officially, he can allow you only one letter per month, and I assume that one will go to your sl... husband."

Hilde chose to ignore her mother's comment. After all, Annie was her only connection to the outside world and the grandmother of her sons. They would need her love and support, however meager it might be, if the worst scenario happened.

"Mother, I know you don't like Q, but could you please send him letters and write news about the boys? He was so thin the last time I saw him, maybe you could also send him some of the food you plan to bring me?"

Annie shook her head. "You want me to help the man who is responsible for my daughter being sentenced to death?"

"Yes. Please, Mother. Do it for me. I will be happy if I know Q is fine."

Annie's nostrils flared. "Why do you still love that man? He's brought nothing but misery to you and your sons."

"I understand that you are angry with him. I really do." Hilde ran a hand through her hair, desperate to make her mother understand. "But yes, I still love him as much as I did throughout our entire life together. If it is even possible, I love him now even more, because only now I know what I had in him and what I will lose with him."

Annie scoffed, but Hilde barreled on...

"Even if I stay alive, there will never again be a

man who means this much to me. If I didn't have the children, I wouldn't want anything but to leave this world behind together with him."

"Well, it looks as if your wish will be granted," Annie hissed.

Hilde ignored her and went on. "Right now, in this very moment, I'm glad that I'm not better off than he is, that we are both in prison, both sentenced to death. He said that those nine years with me were the world for him. The memory of those experiences with me now make it easier for him to die."

Annie lifted her chin. "Is it as easy for you?"

"I agree with him. We have enjoyed the pleasures of life, as much as possible, and we always knew that we were privileged. We had a good life, and we had each other. Never once did we fight or argue, we didn't have unfulfilled desires, were always content and happy, and we have enjoyed this consciously. Few people will be able in their old age to say that they have experienced nine years of pure bliss."

Annie was quiet now, looking down at her shoes, and Hilde thought she saw some hint of emotion on her face.

"Mother, for me, it won't be hard to say goodbye to a world that no longer has Q in it. This may be solace for you, Mother, to know that I will have an easy goodbye and death." Hilde slumped back in her chair. It was true. A world without Q wasn't the same; it didn't appeal to her anymore.

Annie sighed. "Fine. I will write him a letter and send him some food."

"Thank you." Hilde hugged her mother.

Annie moved a step away and smoothed her skirt. "Don't despair, Hilde. *Herr* Müller is still working on your case. He's currently weighing his options, whether it's better to appeal your sentence or ask for clemency."

Hilde nodded. "Yes, I know."

A knock on the door indicated that their hour was over. Annie stood and walked to the visitor's exit. In the door, she turned one last time. "Your half-brother will be conscripted as soon as he turns sixteen in a few weeks."

Hilde waited until she was back in her cell to digest the news about her half-brother and his future. Hitler must be desperate if he started conscription of underage boys.

Usually, they weren't sent to the front lines but used as *Luftwaffenhelfer.* Their main job was to operate flak and help shoot down enemy bombers. A dangerous job that took many lives.

Hilde was afraid for her baby brother, but in the current political climate, she knew that even if she were in freedom, there'd be nothing she could do. All Germans had to help the war effort, whether they wanted to or not. Those who didn't comply faced severe punishment.

Chapter 20

In Plötzensee, Q felt surrounded by goodwill. Compared to his time at the Gestapo headquarters and prison hospital, it was actually pleasant. Even the guards treated the prisoners like humans, much different than the Gestapo brutes had done.

Q had his suspicions that the prison director was not a huge fan of the Nazis. Of course, no such words were ever uttered, but the evidence spoke for itself.

The director could have chosen any kind of man as Q's cellmate, ranging from common criminals, forced laborers from the occupied countries to military prisoners of war. But he chose Werner Krauss. Werner and Q had been convicted in the same trial, and supposedly belonged to the same resistance organization the Gestapo had given the name *Rote Kapelle*, Red Orchestra. As such, it was entirely against the rules to put them in the same cell together.

When Q was told he was allowed one letter every month, he didn't have to think for one second to whom this letter would go. He sat down immediately and poured his soul onto the single sheet of paper he'd been given.

An hour later, he put it in the envelope – unsealed – and wrote Hilde's name on it. He had no idea where she was being held captive and put the word *Gefängnis*, prison, beneath her name. The censors would know where to send it.

His mother-in-law, Annie, had kept her promise to Hilde and sent him a package with food and money. No doubt paid with his own money. The accompanying letter was curt and distant. Q unmistakably read between the lines that she blamed him for Hilde's death sentence.

And she is right. It's my fault that Hilde was arrested. I should have...would have...

Whenever he thought about Hilde's fate, his thoughts went down a vicious spiral. It didn't matter that she'd forgiven him; he would never do the same.

Q broke the train of thoughts and came back to the present, stashing the money in his underwear. It wasn't that he distrusted Werner, but you never knew who might search the cell. A bundle of banknotes would be prone to disappear.

He carefully rationed the money to purchase things he found necessary for his continued sanity. In prison, he'd started smoking. It was a good way to occupy his hands and keep the constant hunger at bay.

But most of the money he spent on *Kassiber*, secret messages, to his family. Today was one of those days, and he stirred from his meanderings when the door to his cell opened.

"You wanted to speak with me," the young officer said quietly, motioning for Q to come closer.

"I have need of paper and a pen," Q answered with an equally low voice.

The officer squinted his eyes and told him the price. Q stuck his hand in his pocket to retrieve a banknote and handed it to the officer, grateful that Annie had relinquished her hatred of him long enough to help him from the outside.

"I'll be back within the hour." The officer took the money and disappeared.

Later that afternoon, with his purchased pen, ink, and paper, he wrote a letter to Annie, thanking her for her benevolence.

The following day, he purchased more paper, and with too much idle time on his hands, he began to jot down his thoughts. His scientific brain needed exercise, and he took up his previous work in the area of plant protection and pest management. Without a laboratory or any kind of material, all he did was think and try to solve the problems in theory. Then he would send his conclusions to befriended scientists and wait for their answer if the theory held up to a practical test.

Werner proved to be a valuable friend and discussion partner. With nothing else to do, they argued about everything under the sun. Despite not being a scientist, Werner always listened intently when Q bounced off his ideas about plant protection. Several times, he made remarks that helped Q to continue with his research.

But Werner also had a project of his own in the works. His mind was as sharp as Q's, just in a different field. As a literary professor, he had full power over words and scathing wits. In the boredom of prison life, he soon started to write a satirical novel that he called *Die Passionen der halkyonischen Seele* – The Passions of a Halcyon Soul.

Q was thoroughly impressed with the ingenuity of the hidden side blows to the Nazi regime. The novel's principal protagonist was an air force officer, and it took Q only the first chapter to find out who'd been the model for the protagonist: Harro Schulze-Boysen.

While Q always teased Werner about his fine arts, he actually loved the idea and enjoyed reading or listening to the chapters as they formed. The hidden messages in the novel were powerful and mundane at the same time.

"When the Nazi's are gone, your book will become a standard work, I'm sure," Q said.

"Oh, this is only the first draft. It must be polished before it will be good," Werner hedged, full of the insecurities of any writer in the world.

"I give Hitler another year or two at most," Q said, choosing to ignore Werner's remark.

"That war is plain crazy," Werner agreed. "And every time they plug a hole in one place, two new ones appear somewhere else. I can't see how Germany can hold up much longer."

Q still wasn't allowed visitors thanks to *Kriminalkommissar* Becker's intervention. But Werner was, and each time he came back from those meetings with a renewed sense of hope.

A hope that the Nazi reign of terror was coming to an end. But would it come soon enough to save them?

Chapter 21

Hilde held in her hands a letter. From Q.

She reverently opened the envelope and pulled out the sheet of paper. Reading his words, her heart filled with love and gratitude while her eyes filled with tears.

My dearest Hilde,

While I'm writing this, my heart is full of eternal love for you. You were the best thing that happened to me, and I couldn't have wished for a better companion. Despite the war and everything else that happened, those were the most wonderful nine years in my life, and I wouldn't want to miss one minute of them.

When my time to leave this earth arrives, I will go grateful and happy to have enjoyed everything a man can ask for. With you.

But at the same time, my soul is riddled with remorse. Words cannot express the depth of my guilt over your fate. It is entirely my fault that you're in this awful situation. It was never my intent to hurt you or cause you any pain and, believe me, I would gladly give my life to spare yours. If I had known the terrible consequences, I would never have asked you to type those fateful papers.

You are with me every waking second of every day. I miss you. Your smile, your sweet voice, your quick wit. Everything. My mind is consumed with thoughts of you.

Hilde stopped reading, and a smile tugged at her lips. She didn't doubt that Q *often* thought about her, but the moment the next technical problem caught his curiosity, he forgot all about the world around him, including her.

It had happened countless times during their time together, and she'd learned to accept it as a part of him. Hilde was convinced that not even his incarceration could change the way his brain worked.

She wiped her eyes and continued to read...

Fate has been a cruel trickster. It has given me what I most desired, then took it away. By my own hand.

Unfortunately, there was no easy way out for us. The powers that be didn't allow us to leave everything behind and start a new comfortable life in America. How I wish that had occurred. Many times, I wondered exactly which powers had an influence? Earthly powers? Celestial powers? Or pure coincidence? Bad luck? We will never know.

Hilde stopped again, wondering what their lives might have been like in America. After a while, she shook her head. Dwelling on what-ifs was counterproductive and would only bring about sadness and depression.

She picked up the letter and finished reading Q's words...

In hindsight, it's easy to see that if we had visited my cousin Fanny in summer 1939 as we had planned, we'd never have returned to Germany because of the breakout of the war.

Now I tend to believe it was more than inconsequential luck. We were meant to stay here. We were meant for greater things. It is just unfortunate that you, my dearest Hilde, got caught up in my destiny and are now paying for my convictions with your life.

My friends and I were fighting for a good cause. For a better world. The world of peace and equal opportunities. A world without war. But destiny had different things in mind.

It seems that the world has still to learn a lesson. A lesson that must include the horrors of war to give way for a better future, of mankind rising like a phoenix from the ashes, when everything that is bad and evil has been burnt down to the ground, and the fire has fertilized the soil for good things to grow.

On the subject of our children, I have every confidence they will be fine with your father and Emma. Volker and Peter love their grandparents, and they will have a happy life with them.

Annie has kindly sent me a package with food and some necessities. If you have the chance to express my thanks to her, please do so.

While I am resigned to my sentence, I still have hope that yours will not be enforced. So many convicted have received clemency. Please stay strong and never lose your inner sunshine.

I'm counting the seconds until I receive your letter. In four weeks from now, you will hear from me again.

My love, until next time. Think of me and know that my love surrounds you and will never die, even if my body does.

Forever,

Q

Hilde wiped her eyes and tucked the letter into her pocket. She touched it whenever she felt lonely and the reality of her circumstances became overwhelming.

One of those days, she and Margit were talking when the male prisoners from the adjacent building had their one free hour in the courtyard. Snippets of conversation floated through the tiny open window inside.

"I'll hang myself if this continues much longer," a male voice said.

"And what with exactly," another voice answered.

"...can't take it anymore...the uncertainty..."

Hilde stood and closed the window. "Pour souls. You wouldn't think so, but the imprisonment is so much harder on the men."

"Just last night, I heard a newcomer scream and clamor in his dreams," Margit added.

When the night was clear and there were no enemy bombers in the sky, the prison walls echoed and amplified even the slightest noise.

"It's not the danger or death lurking around the corner. These are not the bad things. The real bad thing is the uncertainty, not knowing what will happen to you. It's what starts eating you up from the inside. The isolation in the cell. The hunger. Every one of those men over there would rather go to a concentration camp or a real prison than stay one day longer here on death row." Hilde stopped talking when she noticed Margit's pale face. She put an arm around her shoulders. "Don't worry, you'll get out of here."

Margit nodded. "I will. I must."

Later in the afternoon, they heard the sound of breaking glass. It came from across the courtyard and was followed by an eerie wolf-like howl.

"It's from the men's building," Margit stated.

"Yes." Hilde didn't want to think about what exactly had happened and retrieved Q's letter from her pocket. She lifted it to her nose and inhaled deeply, savoring the lingering smell of her husband.

"You adore the letter more than the man," Margit teased her.

Hilde breathed in the scent again and smiled. "I would much prefer the man, but what can I do? This letter is all I have, and so adore it I will."

Chapter 22

Today was Q's fortieth birthday. Q held a letter from his wife in his hands and thought he couldn't have asked for anything nicer this day. He turned the envelope over in his hands for several long moments before he slit it open and withdrew the sheet of paper.

Despite knowing better, he hesitated to read the words. What if she had changed her mind and was angry with him, or condemned him for getting her into this situation? What if she never wanted to write to him again?

His fingers trembled as he smoothed the letter open on his lap. When he could no longer stand the uncertainty, he looked down and began to read...

My dearest Q,

Oh, how my heart rejoiced to receive your letter. I keep it with me at all times and let my fingers caress the paper as if it was your cheek. At night, the letter comforts me in my loneliness, and it is as if you were with me.

I love you with every fiber of my body, and I will always be faithful to the love we share.

Please do not feel guilty about causing my harsh fate. I absolve you from all of it. Yes, I have felt desperate in recent days, but I would never have wanted to forgo the wonderful times with you by my side.

That said, I want you to know that I do not condone your activities against the Reich. If I had known about your intentions, I would have found a way to make you change your mind.

Q stared at the paper in disbelief, the letters dancing in front of his eyes until it dawned on him, and he grinned. Werner wasn't the only person who could write with hidden messages. *Hope you had fun reading this, dear censors.*

He traced his fingers across the paper, bringing Hilde's sweet face back to his memory. He could actually *see* her standing in front of him, one hand on her hip, her blue eyes twinkling with mischief. His heart filled with emotion.

But I want to stay by your side always like I promised on our wedding day. In good times and bad times. In life and until death do us part. None of us are promised only happiness, and I never worried about bad times, because I had you, my love. Although, I didn't expect death to come so soon.

It's funny really. You used to joke about us growing old and doddery. And I imagined us reaching our eightieth year with a multitude of experiences to tell our grandchildren, but it looks like that is not to be.

I hope your health is much improved and that you are finding an outlet for your brilliant mind. Mother Annie is allowed to visit me one hour every month, and I pleaded with her to give you as much help as she wished to give me. As you can imagine, she's not very fond of you at the moment, but I am relieved she did send you some much-needed things.

Even though I know from her that Volker and Peter are fine and healthy with Emma and my father, I worry about them every day. How could a mother not worry when she's separated from her children?

My rational mind tells me that Emma and my father are showering them with love and affection and will do everything to make their harsh fate as bearable as possible, but my heart tells me that only I can give them the motherly love they need.

A smear blurred some letters, and Q sighed. He knew exactly what strained her conscience so much. Hilde had vowed to never let her children suffer the same fate she had. Growing up without a loving mother.

All he could do was repeat over and over that Emma and Carl would do their best until Hilde – by some miracle – was released from prison and was free to return to her children.

I am looking forward to your next letter. Please tell me everything you do, even the tiniest details. It is my only way to be with you and to imagine being by your side.

All my love forever,

Hilde

Q dropped the letter to his lap and closed his eyes. With his inner eye, he re-read her sentences many times and savored the warmth and love in her words. *Hilde is still alive, and she still loves me.* That was all that mattered.

Nobody knew what the future held, or how long it would last, but right now, Q was happy. Hilde's letter was the best birthday present he could have asked for.

Chapter 23

A few weeks later, Hilde had another visitor. Her lawyer, *Herr* Müller, had come to speak with her. She'd not seen or heard from him since the day of her sentencing and wondered what news he would bring.

Hilde did her best to suppress the rising hope, out of fear she might be disappointed. Once again, she found herself in the small visiting room.

"Good day, *Frau* Quedlin," he greeted her with a handshake.

"Good day, *Herr* Müller. What news do you bring?"

"I'm afraid not much," he apologized, but after taking a look at her disappointed face, he hurried to add, "and that is good news. Actually, no news is good news. I was waiting for the dust to settle before making my next move."

"The plea for mercy, right?" Hilde fidgeted in her seat.

"Well, that's what I wanted to discuss with you. I have weighed the alternatives and have come to the conclusion that we should reconsider our original plan to ask for a plea of mercy."

"What? Why?" Hilde asked, not quite following his lengthy sentence.

"In the current political climate, we might have a better chance of success asking for a revision of your sentence. It was unusually harsh, and a more benign judge might reduce it to one or two years of prison."

"You think so?" Hilde's voice was full of hope. Several months ago, two years of prison would have terrified her, but now it sounded like a merciful option.

"I can't promise anything, but it has been done before. It would help, though, if you had influential friends who would support your claim and speak on your behalf. The kind of friends with a party book and rank."

The only person who came to her mind was Erika, who had married the son of an SS-Obersturmbannführer. But Erika's father-in-law was dead and her husband somewhere in occupied France.

"I'm afraid I don't have that kind of friends." Hilde shook her head.

"Unfortunate, but we will proceed on our own then. I believe you have a good case for a revision. There's no real evidence of your involvement in any kind of resistance or sabotage activities."

"I hope so." Her shoulders sagged as she tried to

kindle the spark of hope inside her.

"On a better note, your mother has asked *Kriminalkommissar* Becker for permission to bring your son Volker with her the next time she visits."

Hilde jumped up, excitement burning like fire on her skin. "She did that? When will I see him?"

"He's not yet given a definitive answer, but he seems inclined to grant his permission."

Hilde wanted to throw herself into *Herr* Müller's arms and kiss him. He seemed to suspect some kind of exuberant reaction from her because he clutched his briefcase against his chest warily.

She suppressed the need to cry out in joy, and instead said, "Please give my mother my sincerest thanks for that undertaking."

A relieved expression crossed his face as he retrieved an envelope from his briefcase and handed it to her.

"This is from your mother. You might find it useful." He nodded and bid his goodbyes, the door clicking softly behind him.

Hilde all but danced back to her cell, and in her hurry to tell Margit the good news, she forgot to hide the envelope full of *Reichsmark*. But today was a truly good day because the guard to return her to the cell was the Blonde Angel.

Fräulein Hermann discreetly pointed at the envelope and whispered, "I have to surrender all money to the prison director should I find any."

Hilde quickly coiled up the banknotes and stashed them in her brassiere before handing the envelope over for inspection. She couldn't help but share her elation with the friendly guard.

"Imagine, I might be allowed a visit from my son. Isn't that wonderful?"

"That truly is good news," *Fräulein* Hermann said with a smile.

Hilde never understood why this warmhearted, empathic young woman had chosen such a gruesome profession, but this was not a question she dared ask. Despite her friendliness, Fräulein Hermann still was a guard. No fraternizing with guards allowed.

Back in her cell, Hilde hummed a melody. Life was good. She would see her son. And thanks to her mother, she had *Reichsmark* to buy things. Money made life in prison much more tolerable. It didn't matter that she knew the money was from the estate she and Q had worked so hard to build, nor did it matter that her mother was more than likely taking a large portion for her own needs as well.

All that mattered was that she would soon see her son.

After pestering Margit with endless details and anecdotes about her sons, Hilde sat down to write a letter to Emma. Officially, she was allowed only one letter per month and that one was reserved for Q. But with the stash of money the lawyer had given her, she could afford to pay the guards to smuggle a secret letter outside.

Dear Mother Emma,

Please do not mention this letter in your reply, it wasn't sent through the official channels.

I want to tell you how elated I am that Mother Annie has asked for permission to bring Volker with her during her next visit. I know that you and she never got along very well, and I understand your reasons. Annie can sometimes be difficult to deal with.

A smile twisted Hilde's lips upwards. That would be the understatement of the century. But her intent wasn't to cause more bad blood between her relatives. If the worst scenario should happen, they all had to work together for the best of the children.

I beg you to please try to get along with her, for my sake, and for the sake of your grandchildren.

You will never know the amount of gratitude I feel towards you for taking both of my children under your care. Now that both of your girls are grown enough to not cause you so much trouble, you must now start over again with two little boys who aren't even your flesh and blood. I know they are in the very best hands with you.

But I wish that you will also see to your own health and

your own well-being and ask Annie for help if everything becomes too much for you. She has full power over Q's and my estate and should be able to send money for much needed things like new shoes or clothes.

Peter can wear the handed down things from his brother, but my Volker must have grown since I last saw him, and when spring arrives, he won't fit into last year's clothing.

Please take my sincerest thanks for everything you do. Give my beloved children a big kiss from their mother, and my greetings to Father, Sophie, and Julia.

Your daughter, Hilde

Hilde folded the letter and sealed the envelope, then waited until one of the guards known to deliver secret messages came by and paid her for the delivery.

That night, she fell into a deep sleep filled with happy dreams until the blood curling sound of the air raid sirens made her sit straight up in her bed. Margit already stood, face pale as a ghost, pounding against the cell door.

"Sweetie, there's no use in doing that. You know we have to stay in our cells." Hilde hugged the sobbing Margit. Despite her fierce spirit, she was just a nineteen-year-old girl.

The guards rushed to seek shelter in the basement of the building, while Hilde and Margit crawled under the table and cuddled against each other. This air raid must have been the most terrifying in a long time.

Normally, the thick old prison walls kept most of the noise outside, but today, they creaked and shook as each bomber delivered its deadly cargo onto the city of Berlin.

The minutes crawled and every time Hilde thought it was over, the night sky filled again with the buzzing of approaching enemy aircraft. She'd learned to distinguish the sounds of German flak, a downed British aircraft, and the dreadful bombs.

The impacts approached. After an ear-piercing detonation, crumbs rippled from the ceiling, and glaring light entered through the small window. *Several of the buildings nearby must have caught fire.*

Despite the closed window, Hilde could hear the sizzling and cracking as the fire ate away at whatever was in its path. She just hoped it wouldn't reach the prison. The fire brigade would have other priorities.

The air raid lasted the entire night, and at some time, Margit and she must have fallen asleep coiled together under the table because when Hilde woke from the sudden silence, it was light outside.

While there had been several bombings last year, none of them had done serious damage to Berlin. That changed at the beginning of 1943. Since the start of the year, the constant attacks had become an integral part of life in the capital.

During the next days, the overwhelming power of the attack was the number one topic of conversation amongst prisoners and guards alike. They received word that more than seven hundred people were killed during the bombing and thirty-five thousand rendered homeless due to the destruction of close to a thousand buildings.

The guards told about the utter devastation the bombing had left behind. Rubble wherever one looked. Skeletons of structures stretching out toward the heavens. Entire quarters razed to the ground.

Chapter 24

Q and Werner had grown accustomed to life in prison. Each of them dedicated many hours of the day to their projects. The guards joked about the feverish activities in the cell of those two intellectuals, who actually seemed to enjoy having that much idle time on their hands. But they didn't disturb them, except for the one hour of "leisure" the prisoners had to spend in the backyard.

In the afternoon, they usually argued about every topic under the sun, and once a week, the catholic priest *Pfarrer* Bernau visited their cell to give them moral support.

The priest's main task was to accompany the condemned prisoners during their last hours and give them the last sacrament if they so wished. But apart from that, he made it a habit to visit each prisoner at least once a week and lend an open ear to everyone's sorrows.

Everyone in the prison appreciated him because he never insisted on dwelling on the Catholic doctrine, but took a more humane approach. Regardless of the prisoner's religion, he comforted with words of empathy and friendliness.

Q soon discovered that *Pfarrer* Bernau did a lot more than console. He was an educated man, well versed in theology, sociology, and politics – and a dedicated enemy of the Nazis.

It was an open secret that *Pfarrer* Bernau would help those inmates who couldn't afford to bribe the guards to smuggle secret messages in and out of prison. And, according to rumors, he'd hidden more than one Undesirable from the authorities. God only knew where he got the money, help, and fake papers to carry out his work.

The days passed, and with the infamous Judge Roland Freisler presiding the *Volksgerichtshof,* more and more petty crimes were punished with the death sentence and Plötzensee was literally bursting at the seams.

One day, a young Frenchman called Pascal was put into Q's cell. The lad spoke barely a word of German, but Q did his best to practice his rusty French. Thankfully Werner's French was a lot better, and Q let him do the talking.

Curious about the background of their new cellmate, Werner questioned the young man about the circumstances surrounding his arrest.

"I was hungry. It was cold and dark. That's when I saw a woman with a handbag and stole it from her." Pascal broke out in sobs.

"Why on earth did you do such a stupid thing?" Werner wanted to know.

Pascal explained between sobs, "I don't know. But as soon as I had it, I felt so guilty and threw it away in remorse."

Q couldn't condone his deed. However, stealing a handbag certainly wasn't worthy of capital punishment. There were no words to comfort the young man who was now nearing the end of his life for doing one little stupid thing.

In the next days, more details about Pascal's arrest and trial came to light. Apparently, the court had produced witnesses, in his defense, stating the young Frenchman had rescued two children from a burning building during a recent air raid.

But the judge, one of Roland Freisler's closest followers hadn't cared and given the same punishment a cold-blooded murderer would have received. It was inhumane and unjust.

Even the prison director and most of the employees silently agreed with that appraisal and worked diligently to find reason after reason, no matter how ridiculous, to delay the planned execution.

Pascal was understandably distraught; the language barrier only serving to increase his anxiety and desperation. After his first initial breakdown, he calmed down enough to write his memoirs.

"Now my mother and my girl will at least have a memory of me," he told Q.

Q nodded. What else could he do? He wouldn't start a philosophical discussion in French about how only a conviction to death could bring out the essence of one's life. How being confronted with your imminent death sorted the wheat from the chaff and left you with only the truest, sincerest thoughts about life.

When Pascal was finished writing his memoirs, he begged Q and Werner to promise him they would see that his letters were delivered to his family in Paris after the war.

Werner readily agreed, always optimistic that his death sentence would be revoked, thanks to the generous help from some of his influential friends.

A week later, the executioner came for Pascal.

***

Q wasn't particularly religious, but today he was yearning for *Pfarrer* Bernau's weekly visit. The execution of Pascal had shaken his unstable peace of mind. Once again, the unjust law hadn't known mercy. Not even in this case.

But today, the priest wasn't in the mood for a political argument. Or any kind of discussion.

"What's wrong?" Q asked, running a hand through his curly hair.

"Today was an especially ugly day. One of the

men who died today wasn't at all prepared for it. I did my best to spiritually assist him, but he was so young and didn't want to accept what was about to happen."

"Pascal?" Werner asked, his voice oozing grief.

"It was awful. Yes. He was screaming and kicking and fighting when they placed him on the guillotine. The executioner couldn't do his work, and the Frenchman had to be tied in place. After the deed was done, the hangmen were visibly shaken and told me this was one of the most horrible and unjust executions they'd been commanded to undertake." The priest paused, his emotions clearly visible on his face.

Werner's hands were clenched into fists. "It will be up to the coming generations to judge, but this young Frenchman has led a correct life and one simple mistake during times of turmoil shouldn't have ended it."

The priest made the sign of the cross. "May God bless his soul. And may He help the hangmen riddled with guilt."

"They do have a hard job," Q admitted, shivers of ice running down his spine.

They remained quiet for several minutes before *Pfarrer* Bernau cleared his throat. "I do have more disturbing news from the outside."

"Tell us this news," Werner encouraged him.

"Hitler has commanded the deportation of all Jews from his *Reich*. There have been reports of mass murders during the evacuation of the Jewish ghettos in Poland. Tens of thousands are sent to so-called extermination camps."

"How do you know these things to be true?" Q asked. He didn't doubt for one instant the Nazi were capable of these atrocities, but even to him, it seemed a bit farfetched to deport and kill an entire race. The logistics of transporting and then killing that many people were unheard of.

"I may not disclose my sources, but they have seen it with their own eyes. This is genocide on a large scale. Hundreds of thousands, maybe even a million. Mainly Jews, but also gypsies, homosexuals, God forgive them, mentally ill persons..." the priest made the sign of the cross "...they use gas to kill many people in a short time. Even in my worst nightmares, I'd never feared our government would stoop so low. May God help us, for we are sinners."

"You need to be careful with whom you talk about these things," Q cautioned him. "Not all the prisoners are trustworthy."

"Yes, we have every reason to suspect there are prisoners, even TU, that would turn on you in the hope to save themselves," Werner agreed.

Pfarrer Bernau gave a small smile and knocked on the door to be let outside.

Neither Q nor Werner mentioned the disturbing

information anymore, but deep inside, Q's worry about the state of Germany grew.

How much worse do things have to get before they become any better?

Chapter 25

Hilde had been on pins and needles since she received the official confirmation that her eldest son would be allowed to visit for an entire hour.

When the day finally arrived, Margit helped her comb her hair. They both stared in horror at the bundle of long strands in the brush.

"I'm losing my hair!" Hilde exclaimed. They both knew it was due to a lack of proper nutrition and sunshine.

"No. It's absolutely normal to lose a few hairs every day," Margit lied and added, "You look nice. And your son won't notice."

A few minutes later, one of the guards arrived to take Hilde to the visiting room. Her heart thundered in her throat, and with every step, she became more anxious. *What if he doesn't recognize me? Or doesn't want to see me?* Several times on her path through the long prison hallways, she was tempted to turn on her heels and run away.

Volker had turned three in January and was a bright little boy. Emma told him that his mother was in the hospital and that's why she wasn't allowed to be with him.

Hilde wasn't sure whether she liked that lie or not, but in the end, it wasn't her decision, and Emma insisted it would be better for the boy if he didn't know his parents were in prison. For treason.

The guard opened the door to the visiting room, and Hilde leaned against the doorframe for a moment, gathering her strength. Volker was sitting on Emma's lap, an expectant grin on his face. He looked so grown up Hilde barely contained the tears pooling in her eyes.

She forced a happy smile on her face and called his name, "Volker?"

He turned, and once he saw her, gave a shout of glee, and rushed to throw himself in her arms. Hilde went to her knees and wrapped her arms around his little body, holding him tight until he started wiggling to gain his freedom.

"Mama, are you very sick?" Volker asked.

"I'm much better now. I've missed you so much. Look how much you've grown." Hilde stood up and followed him to the table where Emma sat.

"I'm a big boy, Grandma says so every day." He beamed with pride and started telling so many things, she barely understood a word.

Just hearing his voice made her happy. Hilde reached Emma and embraced her. "Thank you so much for making the trip to bring him here."

"Don't mention it," Emma answered and smiled, gesturing for Hilde to concentrate on Volker.

"Sweetie, can you tell me what you've been doing? How is your baby brother?" Hilde asked and lowered herself to sit on the ground.

"Peter follows me around. Like that." Volker laughed and crawled on all fours across the floor.

"You two are such a good team. Do you play together?" she asked, thinking about how Peter had always imitated his bigger brother and tried to do everything Volker did.

"Sometimes. But he always throws over my building blocks. Can you tell him to stop doing this?" Volker's big blue eyes pleaded with her.

Hilde nodded, her throat closing with unshed tears at the mention of Volker's blocks. Q had made them for him, and they'd been his favorite. It warmed her heart to know that he still played with them.

"I will, sweetie, as soon as I'm with you again. In the meanwhile, you do what Grandma says, yes? And you take care of your little brother for me."

Volker nodded with a serious face and came to sit on her lap. "When are you coming back to us?"

She swallowed hard. "I don't know, sweetie. I hope soon."

"Will you die?" his little voice trembled.

"Oh, my little darling, don't you worry.

Remember that your mother loves you more than anything in the world, and she will always think of you."

"I forgot..." Volker rushed away and came back with a sheet of paper, "I did this for you, so you will get better soon."

She took the drawing and inspected it. Four people standing on green grass. A yellow sun in the sky. And a boat. "That is beautiful, sweetie."

"This is me...and you...Papa and Peter..." Volker beamed with pride as he explained everything he'd drawn for his mother.

Hilde forgot everything around her, and much too soon the guard returned to announce it was time for the boy to leave. She hugged him tightly, whispering words of love in his ear while barely managing to hold back her tears.

"You have fifteen more minutes, I'll watch him meanwhile," the guard said and took Volker with her as Annie entered the visiting room.

It was the first time Hilde had been in the same room with both of her mothers at the same time. An awkward silence captured the place until Hilde finally gained control of her tears. "I'm sorry."

"Don't apologize. I cannot imagine what you're going through," Emma said.

"You have no idea how much his visit means to me. I will cherish this one hour forever in my heart.

Thanks to both of you for making it possible," Hilde said, doing her best to swallow down the tears.

"I did have to pull a few strings, but it wasn't that hard," Annie mentioned and took the second chair at the table.

"Here. I brought you some of the things you mentioned." Emma handed her a package.

Hilde took the package. She'd have a look at it later. Now, she had more pressing issues to discuss with the two women.

"Do you have what you need for the children? Are they safe?"

"The air raids have increased, but they are safe for now. As for what they need...they are growing so quickly. I will soon need a few coupons for shoes and clothing," Emma admitted.

"Annie, unfortunately, this is upon you. With the birth certificate of the children, you can go to the authorities here in Berlin and ask for extra coupons. Then you send them via mail to Emma. And please send her money every month to buy whatever the boys may need."

Annie just stared at her. "Hilde, you think life is easy, but there is no cash left. Your husband hasn't been paid a salary since the day he was arrested, and according to his patent lawyer, royalties are paid once a year only." She sighed and waved a hand. "I checked all your bank accounts, there never was much money. One would think you had been able to save more."

Hilde started to grow angry with her mother. *I'm the one rotting in prison, not you!*

"Then sell a few things, Mother." Hilde scowled. "I'm sure my fur coat would receive a good price."

"Don't be silly, dear. Who would want to buy a fur coat in April?" Annie answered with a roll of her eyes.

Emma had watched the silent fighting with wide eyes and now entered the discussion with a calm voice. "Maybe there's something else from Hilde and Q's estate that you could sell, *Frau* Klein? Silverware, china, or antiques?"

"I will see what is possible and send you money by the end of the week. If you give me a list of things needed, I will also run the errands to receive the extra ration cards. While I may not dedicate too much time to that cause because I have important social obligations to attend to, I will certainly do everything needed for my grandsons," Annie said graciously.

"Thank you, Mother. And couldn't you sublet the apartment in Nikolassee to someone? This way the boys would have a regular income."

"It may be done, but it is a lot of work and hardship," Annie protested, but quickly nodded when she noticed the stern glances of both Hilde and

Emma.

"Time to go," the guard called from the doorway.

Emma pulled a small packet from her purse. "I have some pictures for you of Volker, Peter, and the rest of the family."

"Thank you two so much for taking care of my children." Hilde took the pictures and bid her goodbyes to Emma and Annie before she hurried to the waiting guard, who'd been generous enough to allow Hilde an extra fifteen minutes to speak about organizational details with the two women while she cared for Volker.

Back in her cell, Hilde found Margit waiting to hear every last detail about her visit.

Hilde showed her the pictures Emma had given her. "Look, these are my two cuties. And these are my sisters…" She ran her fingers lovingly over her children's faces and swallowed back a lump in her throat. Seeing her son had been bittersweet.

"What if I never see them again?" she asked Margit through her forming tears.

"You'll be with them again soon," Margit said and hugged her.

Hilde nodded. She wanted so badly to believe it would be true. She smiled at the pictures in her hand and knew she would think back on this one hour with her son every single day while she was here. It would keep her spirits up and help her to stay sane.

Then she opened the package Emma had given her. It contained her favorite pair of black shoes, shampoo, soap, food, a woolen cardigan, two books, and several torn stockings.

"Look, Margit! Finally, I have some comfortable shoes...and shampoo." Hilde opened the bottle and sniffed. "It smells so good."

Margit laughed. "Nothing beats real shampoo. I'm sick and tired of the curd soap they give us."

They scrutinized the food and sat on the lower bunk bed to eat the fresh buns with butter.

"Hmm, real butter," Margit licked her lips, "today is a day to celebrate."

"You know, we're actually quite fine. We have enough to eat, something to read and Emma even sent me work to do. Mending those stockings will keep me busy for days."

"You actually think it's nice of your stepmother to send those torn stockings?" Margit pouted.

"Mother Emma has such a hard life outside, and she works day and night. Caring for my father, her own teenage daughters and now my sons. I feel bad that I can't help more. And I can't find any joy in living such an idle life. At least stuffing stockings will make me feel useful...and keep my hands and mind occupied." Hilde leaned back and took a hearty bite of the fresh bun.

After eating in silence for a while, Hilde spoke

again, "You can't imagine how thankful I am that Mother Annie made the visit with Volker possible. For all her shortcomings, this one deed when it really counted has shown that she does love me."

"Yes, that was nice of her to do." Margit yawned and then asked, "While you're busy mending stockings, can I borrow one of those books you received?"

"Sure, help yourself," Hilde answered with a warm smile. It had been a very good day indeed.

Chapter 26

Q took his daily walk around the courtyard outside, grateful for the one hour of exercise in the sunshine. It was his only reminder of a world outside the prison walls. A faint memory of days spent walking and playing at the lake with his wife and his sons.

Spring had sneaked upon them, and with it, more executions. Just this morning, they had come for two more inmates. They always came in the morning, every day, save for the weekends. Even the executioners worked regular hours.

This awful procedure had become a normal part of daily prison life, and nobody seemed to waste another thought on the morbidity of the situation. Even the hangmen were part of the community and did their best to make a horrific situation more endurable.

It had taken Q a while to come to terms with their habit to walk over to the prisoners for a short chat. But after a while, he came to appreciate the break in routine and trained his brain to separate the "execution business" from his own fate.

"Good afternoon, Doctor Quedlin," one of the

hangmen greeted him. "Do you have a moment?"

"Sure." Q nodded. It wasn't like he had to go anywhere.

"About that Frenchman. It was such a shame we had to behead him. He was a good lad. We actually thought the court would give him mercy, but no such luck. We have to follow the orders of the court, but if someone had asked me..."

"Yes, such a waste of a young life," Q answered. At first, he'd been surprised that hangmen did have a conscience. He'd always envisioned them as cold-blooded monsters, but they weren't. They were just human beings with a horrible job. But they weren't cruel sadists like *Kriminalkommissar* Becker and his men.

The executioners at Plötzensee didn't enjoy their jobs.

"I remember this young man we took a few weeks back," another executioner raised his voice. "He just stood there, sobbing in the death chamber while we finished our discussion on...I don't even recall now. I felt horrible for having made him wait and apologized to him for this very rude behavior."

Just before you killed him, Q added in his mind.

The other executioner joined in the walk down memory lane. "Remember that con man?"

"The one who worked as a hairdresser? He was always smiling and in a wonderful mood."

Q took the bait and asked, "Why was he always in a good mood? He was on death row."

"Yes, but he was actually looking forward to his execution." The executioner chuckled and raised an eyebrow. "Don't you want to know why?"

"Sure. Sounds like a good punch line. Why was he looking forward to his execution?" Q asked.

"Because every prisoner is given six cigarettes to smoke on his last day. He was actually yearning for that day." The hangman burst into boisterous laughter.

"Everyone does what he can to deal with the situation," Q answered and ran a hand through his curls. He wondered how he would behave in his last hours. Would he remain steadfast and unwavering? Or would he crumble and beg for his life?

"Yes. But the civilians have more trouble coming to terms with their death than the military personnel. I remember this Czech colonel who begged us to properly disinfect the guillotine before it was his turn. He didn't want to catch a nasty infection."

There was laughter all around, and even Q broke a smile at that one.

"Sorry, but work calls. See you around," the other one said and waved at Q.

Q bid his goodbyes, hoping he'd be around for a while longer. After the leisure hour, he and Werner were summoned to the prison director's office.

During his time in prison, Q had discovered that the director was a well-educated man who enjoyed a good discussion about science and literature. Not many inmates could provide this.

Q had the suspicion that whenever the cruelties of his jobs became too much, the prison director sent for him and Werner to occupy his mind with lighter material. They would discuss the classic German literature books found in the prison library, like Goethe's *Faust* or Schiller's *The Robbers*, carefully steering clear of any comment about current politics.

But today, the director wasn't engaged in the discussion. After a while, he interrupted them with a sigh. "You might be interested to hear that even the most loyal citizens are turning their back on our *Führer*. Last week, two assassination attempts on Hitler failed."

Q's head snapped around, staring at the director in disbelief.

Werner found his voice first, "Have they arrested those involved?"

The director shrugged. "Maybe. The Gestapo arrested Hans von Dohnanyi and Dietrich Bonhoeffer."

"From the *Abwehr*?" Q asked in disbelief. Since when did the Gestapo arrest *Abwehr* agents?

"Yes. Apparently, they have plotted against our *Führer*, and at least Dohnanyi has forged papers to help several Jews flee to Switzerland. An unimaginable deed," the director said, but somehow Q had the suspicion he actually condoned their doings.

He would never say so openly, but with every day that passed, Q's conviction grew that the director hadn't believed in the Nazi ideology for the longest time. There still was hope for an upheaval from within. If only the silent majority took a stand and fought against their leader.

Chapter 27

Hilde had adapted to prison life, and in Margit, she'd found a wonderful companion. Letters were the highlight of her otherwise boring life in prison, and any day she received one was a happy day.

Mother Annie rarely wrote, but Mother Emma, her mother-in-law, Ingrid, and her sisters, Julia and Sophie, took turns in writing, and she usually received two letters per week.

"I spoke with the Blonde Angel this morning," Margit said with a teasing tone.

Hilde looked up from her needlework into Margit's expectant face. She took the bait. "And what did she tell you?"

"Good news. Very good news," Margit teased.

Hilde knew she had to play her game if she wanted to know what the Blonde Angel had said. "Come on Margit, please tell me."

"I might or I might not..."

Hilde laughed and threw one of the stockings she had just mended at her. "You're as eager to tell me as I'm to hear it."

Margit pouted but then broke out in laughter.

"Got me there. So, the big news is...ta-da... women are not executed any longer."

"They aren't executing women?" Hilde stared in disbelief at her cellmate, as hope spread throughout her chest once again.

"It's not official, but apparently, the executioners are swamped with work, and it was decided to stop executing women for the time being."

"That indeed is good news." Hilde took Margit by her shoulders and danced with her around the tiny cell.

The days trickled by, and every day, more concerning news from the outside reached the prison. The Eastern front had all but crumbled, and the Soviets seemed to gain footing, while the British and Americans had started a Combined Bomber Offensive, a strategic bombing campaign to disrupt the German war economy, reduce the morale, and destroy the housing of the civilian population. Rommel's Afrika Korps had to surrender in Tunisia. One hundred and fifty thousand German soldiers and one hundred and twenty-five thousand Italian soldiers became prisoners of war, and the absence of their manpower had a crippling effect on every other front.

One month had passed since Volker's visit when Annie visited again.

"You look very good, Hilde," Annie said.

Hilde sighed and shook her head. "What do I care about looks?"

"It is important, even in your situation, and I'm glad you're taking care of yourself. Do you need more shampoo?" Annie touched her carefully backcombed hair.

For the first time, Hilde noticed the grey strands in her mother's hair and the profound wrinkles around her eyes.

"No, thanks, but I could use some food. They have reduced our rations again. The only reason I'm not losing much weight is because I barely move."

"Well...what do you do in here all day?" Annie asked, raising an eyebrow.

"Not much. I think what I miss most about being in here is having work to do. Maybe you could bring me some clothes for the children that need to be mended, or some yarn so I could knit them sweaters...anything to keep my hands busy."

"I think I could send you some yarn," Annie said noncommittally. Hilde could feel something was bothering her.

"Don't worry about me, Mother. I don't deny that sometimes I am about to break down, but generally, I'm fine. There's a little window in my cell through which the sun has been shining for weeks. It's been getting warmer each day, and I can see the trees beneath my window. They are blooming green with leaves."

"Yes, the spring is the only good thing we have right now," Annie complained.

"Mother, we should be grateful for what we have," Hilde scolded her. "The weather is so wonderful. Some days, all I can think about are the children and how much they must enjoy being able to get outside and soak up the sun after this long and harsh winter. Even though I can't be with them, I am happy to know they are happy."

"You can say that because you are safe in here, but outside...the constant air raids are demoralizing," Annie said, her face frowning in consternation. "Not one night goes by when we don't have to rush to the shelter. I always worry whether I will survive the night, the lack of sleep has taken its toll on my health and youthfulness, and even my best contacts can't get me real coffee anymore."

Hilde was torn between rage and amusement about her mother's grievances. Here she was, sentenced to death, and Annie complained about *her* hardships? Some things never changed.

"I really don't understand why the British have to make our lives so difficult! Why don't they go back to their island and leave us in peace? I haven't done anything, so why do I have to bear their wrath?"

Hilde chose not to answer and instead directed their discussion back to happier topics. "How is your husband? What opera is he currently singing in?"

"Oh my God, Hilde, sometimes I ask myself, how you can care so little about other people? How do you not know that my poor Robert has suffered from a severe inflammation of his vocal cords and hasn't been able to perform most of the winter? It's all the fault of those bloody British. They destroy everything!"

Hilde sighed and was actually glad when the guard announced their visiting time was over.

Chapter 28

Q's eyes shot daggers at Werner as he paced the tiny cell. Three long strides. Turn. Four small strides. Turn.

"I can't believe you gave away all your inventions to the Soviets. A government never understood," Werner said.

"That's not true," Q protested. "Communism is the only form of government to look out for its people. The reign of the people, no more elites, no more rich persons taking everything for themselves."

"And where did you get your information? You don't seem to know the first thing about this so-called Socialism." Werner stepped into Q's way.

Q scowled. "I can't think when I have to stand still. Get out of my way."

"Oh, oh, the mighty Doctor Quedlin is thinking. But you should stick to natural science, where you are a true creative force and leave political sciences to others. Your philosophy of life is heavily skewed." Werner smirked and stepped aside.

"Oswald Spengler," Q said and ran a hand through his hair, "His book *Decline of the West* explains everything there is to know about the clash of civilizations."

"Phaw...Spengler was wrong," Werner declared.

"How so?" Q queried. "All humans are created equal and if everyone is working for the best of the community–"

"That isn't Socialism, my friend." Werner shook his head.

Q looked towards the window, having heard this before. "So, you would argue against his idea that all civilizations go through a natural life process of birth, growth, maturity, and then death? That all civilizations have a limited lifespan; one that can be predicted?"

"The end of civilizations is not a foregone conclusion. And Socialism is not the capitalism of the lower classes. In my opinion, Socialism is about improving the community by everyone working equally, and ensuring that everyone is reliant on the government to the same degree and the government determines how that community will thrive."

"That's nit-picking," Q said with a smile and continued to present Spengler's important assumptions about the history of civilizations and the interaction between man and his surroundings.

Werner in turn, picked every single argument apart, trying to contradict Spengler with theories of other important philosophers. Their argument continued well into the evening until they both had sore throats from too much talking.

Q was never sure if Werner really believed everything he said about Socialism and Spengler, or if he was simply arguing for argument's sake, as a way to shorten their long prison days. Be it as it might, Q cherished their day-filling arguments and carefully avoided to agree with Werner even on the most insignificant point.

Sometimes *Pfarrer* Bernau joined their discussions, and some of their favorite topics were pedagogic and educational questions. The re-education and de-Nazification of all Germans, and especially the younger generation would have to become first priority after the complete destruction of the German state.

Those questions would determine and influence the entire economic concept of the new Germany. At that point in time, Q had bid farewell to his previous belief that Germany would be able to escape the evil clutches of Hitlerism with its own force, while Werner – of course – clung to the illusion of a revolution from within to overthrow the current government.

"It doesn't matter which way Hitler is thrown from power," *Pfarrer* Bernau said with a stern face, "either way the whole country will be in ashes."

To that statement, unfortunately, everyone had to agree. What they didn't agree on, was how an ideal

German state could be formed after the defeat.

Q partook in this discussion with mixed feelings because he was fully aware that he wouldn't be part of that new country. But maybe Werner and *Pfarrer* Bernau would.

Chapter 29

Hilde should have been grateful, but she wasn't. Today was April 20, 1943, and to celebrate Hitler's birthday, he had generously allowed every prisoner to write an additional letter to a family member. Unfortunately, Q wasn't one of the *approved* recipients because he was a prisoner himself.

She scowled at the blank sheet of paper in front of her and made a face. So now she should be grateful to the man she despised most in this world. The man who was ultimately the cause of her death sentence and unspeakable suffering for millions of people.

"Aren't you going to write that letter?" Margit asked as she stuffed her hastily written words into the envelope.

"Ha. Why can't I write to Q? And why does *this man* give me a present at all? It's his damn birthday, not mine!" Hilde scribbled a skull on the paper.

"Come on, Hilde. You are the person who spends all of her money on smuggling out secret letters, rather than buying things for herself. It would be rather stupid not to seize the opportunity to write an official letter."

"I guess you're right," Hilde sighed and crossed out the skull. Then she started to write a letter to Emma.

My dear mother,

I'm wishing every one of you a very happy and peaceful Easter. The children will be joyful and happy, and you will take joy in them and with them.

I will think a lot about you, and I will imagine how the boys are searching for Easter eggs. Your place is perfect for that kind of game, and I remember how well Daddy can hide the eggs. We used to seek them for hours.

Last year, Q and I searched Easter eggs at our place, and little Peter was just one month old. Meanwhile, my sweetie will be able to walk alone, after what you wrote me in your last letter.

How much I would love to see him! I will never be able to make up for missing his first steps. His first words, it is both cute and unique how a baby starts talking. And everything else he has learned.

And he already learned a song! How much I yearn to see him clapping his little hands while humming the melody to Backe, backe Kuchen. If I will ever see him again, then all of this has passed.

It's terrible that he got the measles as well and you had to care for another sick child. I always am afraid that it is too much for you. I know how much work the two boys make, and how cranky they are when they get all the childhood diseases. Of course, always both of them. I hope your health will cope with this burden.

But I am so grateful that the children can be with you and don't have to go to an orphanage. And give my thanks to Sophie for making clothes for them.

Can I help somehow? If you send me material and patterns, then I can sew by hand. Or when Sophie has made little pants, maybe I can embroider them? I still have so much yarn at home it would give me the biggest joy to do some work for the children and help you out. Please ask Mother Annie to send me some, and don't forget to send me the measurements of the children. I have no idea how much they have grown. It's been such a long time...

You can have all the shoes I still have in our apartment. You wear the same size as I do and this is the least I can do for you to show how grateful I am for all your work. In these days, good shoes are a fortune, and you deserve them.

Can I give you something else from my things? Or to your daughters? Just tell me what you need, and Mother Annie will send it to you. You have to endure enough hardship by taking care of my children, I want to help in whatever small ways I can.

Mother Annie sent me a huge chunk of sausage. Were those the coupons from you? Many thanks for it, it is wonderful! But I didn't want to have those special foods because I wanted Mother Annie to send them to Q. He needs it so much more than I do.

Soon, it will be Julia's and your birthday. I'm sending you my best wishes right now because I never know when

I'll be able to send another message.

I have told Mother Annie, if she travels to the Baltic Sea in the summer, she should take the children with her. Would you allow that? It would be a lot of fun for them.

For now, I'm sending you my best wishes for the new year in your life. All my greetings to you, Dad, Sophie, and Julia.

And one thousand kisses to my little sweethearts!

Love, Hilde

Hilde drew a birthday cake with candles below her signature and carefully folded the letter and stuffed it into an envelope. Then she dabbed at her eyes. Thinking about her children was joy and torture at once.

"I wish I could send my sons something for Easter," Hilde murmured.

"You and your children…" Margit teased her.

"You'll understand when you're older and have children yourself." Hilde got up and knocked on the door to indicate she was finished writing. A guard showed up and received both of their letters.

Margit shook her head. "I doubt I will ever have children. Not in a world like this one."

"Don't you want a family? What about your parents? I'm sure they want that for you?"

"You don't know my family." Margit knitted her

brows together.

Hilde gave her a stern look. "That's right. I don't because you never talk about them. You know everything about my family, and I know nothing about yours." Hilde had tried several times to get Margit talking, but this was the one topic she was very tight-lipped about.

"You really want to know?"

Hilde smiled and nodded.

"My father is an important man in the Gestapo, and my mother is a good German housewife and mother." Margit made a face. "My two brothers are officers in the Wehrmacht and my sister is the leader of her *Bund Deutscher Mädel* group. I'm the black sheep of the family."

"What did you do? You've never told me."

Margit scowled and spit on the floor. "I hate the Nazis and their stupid racial ideology…"

Hilde kept quiet as Margit paused, deep in thought. The turmoil on the younger woman's face was apparent. It would be good for her to get whatever was hurting her out in the open.

"…I fell in love with the son of our neighbors. My father was livid. Not because I kissed that boy, but because he was a *Mischling!*"

Hilde put her hand over her mouth. The daughter of a Gestapo officer and a half-Jew. Of course her father was angry.

The expression on Margit's face turned from angry to pained, and she continued with a low voice, "...the next day, he and his mother had disappeared, and nobody would tell me what happened. I was grounded for two weeks, and then my father decided to send me away to a training camp with the *Bund Deutscher Mädel*..." Margit's face brightened, and a mischievous gleam entered her eyes. "But I wouldn't budge. I explicitly told our leader what I thought about that whole charade."

Hilde couldn't hold back a giggle. She could vividly imagine exactly what Margit had said to the BDM leader. Hilde might have done the same thing ten years ago.

"My father was summoned, and it created quite a scandal for him. So, he decided to teach me a lesson and had me arrested."

"You can't be serious," Hilde exclaimed. Although, on second thought it might be true. Margit's family visited her often, and after every visit, her mood was abysmal.

"I am dead serious. Father says I'll be released the day I publicly repent and swear to be a good German girl like my sister."

Hilde stared at her with wide eyes.

In the following weeks, Hilde and the other prisoners relentlessly worked to convince Margit that she should fake remorse to get out of prison.

"It won't do any good if you rot away in here," Hilde said, "think about how much more good you can do when you are outside and work in the underground. I'm sure some of the women in here can arrange contacts for you."

Several days later, Hilde received notice from her lawyer that her petition for a revision of the sentence had been denied. She sighed as her hopes to receive lifelong imprisonment in lieu of the capital punishment were shattered. *Herr* Müller assured her he would not give up and would now issue a plea for mercy. It was a faint hope, but it was all she had.

And if this wasn't enough to dampen her mood, Margit brought worrisome news after another visit from her family.

"France is sending four hundred thousand *voluntary* workers to help the Reich make up for the German men that have been sent to the front. My father says there are over one and a half million prisoners of war earning their keep and doing valuable labor for the regime." Margit spat on the floor. "Nazi bastards."

"So many lives ruined...poor soldiers. When will this awful war be over?" Hilde said on a sigh. Some days she just couldn't take it anymore. On those days, death actually looked like a desirable option.

"My father didn't say much about the war. It seems the Allies are advancing against the *Wehrmacht*, but Hitler announced that Berlin is now free of Jews and that the rest of Germany – indeed, the entire Reich – will soon follow suit."

"All Jews? Everywhere? Where are they going? The camps?" Hilde's eyes widened to the point she feared they would pop out.

"Yes." Margit nodded absent-mindedly. She seemed to be absorbed by her own worry about her half-Jewish boyfriend.

"Is it true, the rumors about what happens in those camps?" Hilde whispered.

Margit glanced at Hilde and pressed her lips together. "I don't know for sure, but I spied on my father a few times, and I'm almost positive Jews are killed in those camps. I overheard him talking about how they have developed a *wonderful* way of killing many unsuspecting people in a short amount of time."

Hilde shuddered. "There are over ten million Jews in Europe. He can't kill them all. That's just not possible."

Chapter 30

May had arrived, and Q sat in his cell scribbling notes when one of the guards opened the door. "You have a visitor."

Q looked up, sure the guard was talking to Werner, but Werner wasn't in the cell. "For me?"

"Yes. Let's go."

Q followed the guard, wondering who the visitor could possibly be. His lawyer wasn't due for another few weeks, and *Kriminalkommissar* Becker had made it very clear that Q didn't deserve to receive visits from friends or family.

When he saw the woman waiting for him in the visitation room, his jaw practically fell to the ground.

"Annie?" Q asked in case she was an apparition, then moved forward to shake her hand, but she waved him away.

"I'm not here to make nice. You are the reason my daughter is sitting in a prison cell facing a death sentence. It's all your fault."

"It's nice to see you, too," he said when she paused in her tirade, "and I can't thank you enough for the money and food you have been sending me."

"For me, you could rot in hell, but Hilde begged me to send you packages," Annie clarified, "I have no idea why this woman still loves you after everything you did to her."

Q wanted to protest, but thought better of it and let her vent. There was nothing to be gained by arguing with Annie when she was like this. And what could he say in his defense? He had incurred the heavy guilt by causing pain to the person he loved most in the world.

"How did you receive permission to visit me?" he asked when Annie had finished accusing him.

"The lovely *Kriminalkommissar* Becker is a man who knows how to distinguish right from wrong – unlike my son-in-law," Annie said with a complacent smile.

Q nodded, although his opinion about Becker didn't quite match hers. "Give the *Kriminalkommissar* my best regards and tell him I'm grateful he allowed your visit. But I reckon you didn't go to all the trouble to remind me of my guilt in Hilde's fate."

"That's right, I didn't." Annie nodded. She pulled some papers from her purse and laid them in front of him. "I want you to sign these."

Q looked at them briefly. "What are they?"

"These papers will sign custody of your children over to me," Annie said and tapped on them.

Q stepped back as if struck. "No. I won't sign

these. Hilde and I have already decided that Gunther is to have custody of our boys."

"Your brother? The man who repels Hilde like the devil hates holy water? You cannot be serious," Annie shrieked, clearly furious at his denial.

"I am serious. Gunther will be the custodian." Q folded his hands in an attempt to keep his calm.

"You can't honestly think your brother is a suitable custodian for two young boys? He's a socialist for God's sake."

"Socialist or not. He's a good citizen in good standing with the authorities, and he's a lawyer. He knows about all the administrative things to be kept in mind. Furthermore, I've written to Gunther and expressed Hilde's and my explicit wish that my boys will be sent to live with my cousin Fanny in America as soon as the war is over."

Annie paled, and it took her a few moments to gain her voice again. "You would send your innocent children into enemy territory?"

"The American are not our enemies. The Nazis are the enemy."

"That thinking is what has landed you in this position." Annie sneered at him. "When we have won the war, there won't be any Americans left to send your children to. They will be better off in Germany."

Q groaned inwardly. Apparently, some people

still believed that Germany would win this war. It escaped his grasp how someone could be that stupid.

"I'm not giving you custody of my children. This is my last word."

"Well then, I should leave," Annie said and extended her hand. A wave of nausea caught him as he noticed the diamond ring on her finger. Hilde's wedding ring.

"That ring belongs to my children, not to you," he said in a tightly controlled voice.

"It's not needed for their care at the moment, so there's no reason I can't wear it," Annie moved her hand until the diamond caught a ray of sunshine and reflected it a million times. A pattern in all colors of the rainbow appeared on the otherwise dull grey walls.

"You could sell it and put the money aside for the boys," Q said, not taking his eyes off the ring.

"Not right now, we wouldn't get much money for it. Thanks to your friends, Germany is in such a bad shape that nobody wants to buy diamond rings, or any kind of jewelry for that matter."

"Still, that ring belongs to Volker and Peter."

"And I'll see that they get it, but after the war. Right now, it's better to keep things like this hidden, and what better place to hide it than on my finger?" Annie asked him.

Q knew he wasn't in a position to do anything

about her abusing her control of his wealth. She could do whatever she pleased, and all he could do was sit around and watch. It rankled deeply and strengthened his conviction to give custody of his boys to Gunther and not to her.

As Annie left, he said, "I'm not sorry about what I did, because I still believe it was the right thing to do, but I'm truly sorry that I dragged Hilde into this. Please know that I love your daughter with all my heart and soul."

Chapter 31

Hilde sat down to write her monthly letter to Q. As always, his wellbeing and that of their children was uppermost in her mind.

Emma had recently sent her pictures of the boys, and she tried to decide which one to send to Q. He'd be so happy.

My dearest Q,

I wonder how much longer I shall be able to write you. Things have become almost normal here, as odd as that might sound. Emma has sent me two pictures of our darling boys, and I have included one of them here for you to see.

It's unbelievable how fast they have grown, and even harder to imagine that they were taken from me almost half a year ago.

My visit with Volker was so precious, and I think of that hour with him every single day. I wish you would be allowed to see him, too, but alas, I fear you may never see them again.

Annie visits me every month.

Hilde paused. It wouldn't be wise to write about Annie's constant whining about the hardships in her life, or how she used the situation to her own benefit. Then Hilde smiled and took the pen again...

You know her; she's such a good soul. Always putting the wellbeing of others above her own. She never complains when Emma asks her to send much-needed funds for the boys' upkeep. Apparently, she had to sell a few of our things because there wasn't enough cash and I convinced her to sublet our apartment in Nikolassee for the time being. I hope this is in accordance with your wishes.

Are you receiving the packages I asked Annie to send you? I told her I will gladly do without anything as long as I know that you are well. You need the extra food so much more than I do.

Thankfully, my health is decent, and I haven't lost much weight because I spend all day sitting in my cell on the bed, day in and day out. Such an idle life is not something I enjoy, and I long to be useful. Annie and Emma both send me small tasks to do. But the mending, stuffing, and knitting is always finished within a few days, and I have nothing to do but sit and wait for the next package, write letters when allowed, and wish for better days.

Hilde ran a hand through her dull, lifeless hair and looked in horror at the bundle of hair between her fingers. Q had always loved her shiny hair. If she continued to shed like a cat in spring, she'd soon be bald.

Memories of better times formed in her mind. Their honeymoon in Italy, a blissful time without worries. She gave a deep sigh and continued her letter.

We had such a good life together, and I wanted to thank you for each and every day. I miss you and our boys more than anything, but the good memories of our time together give me solace. Please know that you are always on my mind, and no matter what the future holds, my love for you is eternal. I wouldn't have wanted to miss one single day with you, and I gladly endure everything if this is the prize I have to pay for nine years of bliss.

How many people can say they lived life to the fullest? Those nine years with you mean more to me than a lifetime without you could. My life turned around the day I met you, and from then on I was the happiest person on earth.

Hilde placed a kiss on the paper, and for lack of lip color, she traced the shape of her lips with the pen. When she was content with her artwork, she took the pen one last time to finish her letter.

You are probably busy putting down all sorts of thoughts on paper, and I hope that one day they will fall into the right hands. I love your brilliant mind. I love everything about you.

Your Hilde

Margit waited until Hilde had finished her letter and then pointed to the pictures lying on the mattress next to her. "Your boys are so cute."

"Yes. Aren't they? Volker is the spitting image of his father with his blond curls, but Peter takes after me." Hilde grinned. "Look, he's finally growing some hair. You can see it's dark and will be straight like mine." She handed Margit the pictures.

"They look happy," Margit commented.

Hilde fingered the pictures when Margit returned them. "My heart hurts at the thought of giving one of the pictures away, but I want Q to have one as well. So he will know what our children look like now."

"I'm sure he'll be very appreciative," Margit said.

"I'll ask Emma to replace the one I sent him, then I'll have both pictures again," Hilde murmured.

Margit laughed at her. "You and your children. I wish I could meet them one day. By the way, isn't your stepmother writing to Q as well and could send him pictures?"

"I know she is writing him, but he cannot answer her because he is only allowed one letter every four weeks and he saves that letter for me. Apparently, sending secret messages is more difficult in his prison."

"We are lucky," Margit agreed.

"I'm not so sure I can agree wholeheartedly," Hilde answered and got up from the bed. She was away from her children with only a few words and a picture here and there to keep her abreast of their growth. She wasn't tucking them into their beds at night or taking walks in the park with them. She wasn't lucky. She was on borrowed time and barely surviving.

Was this a unique form of torture? It certainly wasn't luck.

"You know what I mean," Margit said, and after a look at Hilde's nostalgic face, she added, "Let's go for a walk."

Hilde looked at her cellmate, pondering whether the girl had completely lost her mind now, but Margit linked arms with her, and they went for a walk in their cell. Five steps, turn, another five steps, turn, while Margit pretended they were walking outside in the park and Hilde's boys were with them.

"Look how big they are! Hasn't Peter grown since our last walk? And the way he's talking. His little voice is so sweet."

Hilde giggled, and for lack of a better pastime she went along with Margit's game. "Oh yes, he walks like a big one. And he looks just like his brother did at his age. Aren't they wonderful?"

"Yes, they are."

Hilde turned and looked at her cellmate. "I remember as if it had happened yesterday how Volker walked his first steps alone between his dad and me. A few steps from one to another. We were sitting opposite each other, and for his safety, we had put out our arms to the left and right of him. But he managed all on his own, he was so proud and beamed all over his cute little face."

Hilde became serious again. "I'll ask Emma to cut a lock from their hair and send it to me."

"I'm sure she will. You're lucky to have someone like your stepmother to take care of your boys. Many women who get arrested don't have that luxury and their children are sent to the orphanages or to the workhouses." Margit stopped walking, slightly out of breath.

"I really am thankful. They could nowhere have a better life than with their grandmother. My parents have a small garden attached to their house where the children can play outside."

"When I was a child, we often visited my aunt in the countryside, and I loved running around outside. We would wake up extra early, and my sister and I would rush out to explore."

"Peter is the one who wakes up early every morning…" Hilde murmured.

"Oh yes. As soon as they are awake, small children believe everyone else has to get up with them. I have enough nieces and nephews to know."

Their happy chatter was interrupted by the guard who came to bring them dinner and reminded them of their harsh reality.

Chapter 32

As May 1943 progressed, Q thought of a plan to save Hilde and asked for permission to send a letter to Hermann Göring, the head of the Luftwaffe who was also responsible for all military production by means of the four-year-plan, in addition to his monthly letter to Hilde.

While he was waiting for his request to be decided upon, he initiated Werner and *Pfarrer* Bernau into his plan during one of their weekly chats.

"*Pfarrer* Bernau, I wonder if I might run an idea past you?" Q started the conversation.

"Certainly. What's on your mind?" the gaunt man in his fifties answered.

"I was working on the development of a new secret weapon prior to being arrested. *Horchtorpedos*, or acoustic torpedoes, aim themselves by listening for the sound of a ship's screw. When I was still involved, we had a prototype called *Falke*, but it turned out too susceptible to faults. It often picked up other sounds and aimed for them, missing the target. Anyhow, I think I've solved the problem."

"And..." *Pfarrer* Bernau said and tilted his head.

"Well, here is my plan. I have been asked for permission to send a letter to Hermann Göring. I will offer him my solution about how to make the *Horchtorpedos* foolproof in exchange for him securing a life prison sentence for Hilde instead of the death penalty."

"That is a bold move," the priest said with a serious face.

"What makes you think he would go for this? Those torpedoes won't do much good in this war, it's too close to being finished," Werner commented.

"That's what we believe, but our government still thinks it can win this war, and they need the *Horchtorpedos* to work reliably." Q coughed a bitter laugh. "Those delusional men in power always believe a new invention or more advanced model of something that already exists will be the holy grail to victory."

"But you would condemn your wife to life in prison. Would she want this?"

Q shook his head, "Hitler's regime won't last forever..."

"They are calling for a thousand year Reich," *Pfarrer* Bernau reminded him.

"Yes, but we know that will never stand. At some point, the masses will either dwindle to the point the regime couldn't keep up, or they will revolt in great numbers," Q argued.

"The people are too trodden down to even think about that kind of revolt," the priest reminded him softly, everyone having kept their voices down because of the nature of their discussion.

"I think you should do it, what is the worst that could happen?" Werner asked.

"...that my solution actually works," Q whispered, his conscience screaming to be heard.

Pfarrer Bernau put his hands on Q's shoulders and looked into his eyes. It felt disturbingly like facing the Last Judgment. "That, my son, is a dilemma only you can decide. Consider your decision carefully, and may God be with you in every step."

Q spent most of the night and the next day thinking. Was Hilde's life worth more than the lives of uncounted nameless sailors who might be killed by the *Horchtorpedos* Q had helped to improve? Was her life worth betraying his own ideals and convictions to never harm anyone? But if he didn't try to save her, how could he forgive himself for killing what he most loved in the world?

He pressed his lips into a tight line. *It's too late to use the Horchtorpedos in this war anyway. Nobody will be hurt.*

It was a lie. And he knew it.

The next day, his request for a letter to Göring was granted, and he sat down to write his offer. There was still a chance Göring wouldn't take him up on it.

Chapter 33

Q was growing maudlin as he waited day in day out for the executioners to come for him. Similar to the young Frenchman, he sat down to write what he considered his "legacy."

My dear little mother,

Just before Whit Sunday, while cleaning my cell, I received the letter you wrote on June 6. I was so delighted and moved that I, the cleaning rag still in hand, broke out in screams of joy, of consent, and of blessing.

Of course, I have read your letter many times since, and the need to tell you my inner thoughts became so strong that I asked for an additional letter, which was thankfully granted to me. The one letter I am normally allowed always is reserved for Hilde. For her, it means so much, maybe everything.

How friendly the act of the grace of the gods that I may still while alive receive an earthly manifestation of your love coming to me in the form of a simple piece of paper written by your hand. Yes, I can feel your love around me, helping and blessing me.

Oh, if I could describe to you what inner joy, what paradox, inexplicable and elated vibrancy, what preparedness for my fate has filled me.

What a peace!

How all those long and silent hours in prison have become a present, if I spend them meditating. Which I never had the time before, or better, I never took the time to do.

But first, I want to clarify something just in case, even though I don't think this is necessary with you. All those spiritual goods that I still receive, all the maturity and rounding my soul receives, the goal of your blessing and that of the god's themselves: they are not meant in case of me staying alive (how kitschig that sounds) of being rescued from death, and will be rendered senseless with my execution. No, I take everything with gratitude and happiness as a win in the clear certainty that I will soon finish my life here.

A small joke may clarify my opinion for you...some poor guy has painted the walls of the cell with sentences like "Virgin Mary, please rescue me for the sake of my family" or "Mother of mercy fullness, please lead everything to the good end" and so on.

Under one, "God be with me," I could not resist scribbling behind that sentence: "he is with you, but that doesn't impede him to let you die here through the guillotine."

And is not my current situation, seen in the right light, a unique chance that I will not slide into death without a warning? Will not be a laggard in the sense of "tomorrow is another day," but through the certainty that within a foreseeable time my life will be over. I am eager to make each minute count and gather as much spiritual awareness as I can.

Everything in my cell is geared towards helping me to gain the most spiritual awareness. Look, from one moment to the next, I have been freed from all those mundane tasks like earning money, going shopping, household chores, and of work that was mediocre at best, but has used up many hours of my day. (My work at Loewe was due to the war way below or besides my interests.)

In prison, life is isolated and pre-designed. Every day is like the last, and the next one will just be like today.

Long refreshing hours of sleep and rest, food that is very simple but not worse than the food the free people in the war-ridden country eat, punctual meals, and once a day a short walk, good discussions with other prisoners, and even the luxury of reading good literature.

We have valuable books at our disposal. I just read Wilhelm Meister's Apprenticeship, Italian Journey, and Götz von Berlichingen by Johann Wolfgang Gothe. Selma Lagerlöf, the Swedish literature Nobel Prize winner, and Eduard Mörike.

And as a special favor for me, I am allowed to work scientifically, writing down all my inventions, ideas, and experiences. Furthermore, I am debriefing my three years of work at the Biologische Reichsanstalt in the field of plant protection.

All of you spoil me and make it easy for my soul to say goodbye. Hilde sends me heroic letters, full of love, where she repeats her unwavering love for me and forgives me, despite my actions. Those actions that caused so much pain not only for me but for her and our two children.

She absolves me from the guilt of having caused her own misfortune, pain, and death threat. And in eternal love and connection, she wants to share my fate without quarreling if it is deserved or undeserved.

What a wonderful life partner I have had. I see this more than ever now in bad times. Please think of her with the same love you think about me.

How amazingly well the children seem to be cared for. I can think only the most joyful and hopeful thoughts about them. Your letter has elated me. That you love my Volker so much that you would take him as your own. And the wonderful Dremmers.

My body is through the mercy of the gods completely healthy, no aches and pains hurt me.

Then my cell. I believe I'm made for prison life, for living in a small cell. Haven't you had a vision of me from a former life, where I have been writing in a cell?

I don't feel locked in or encaged. No, I feel safe and secure inside my cell, and the small confinements of the physical room give me the needed focus to concentrate on my spiritual development.

But I am still attached to my earthly life and can appreciate the small patch of sky that I can see through the window of my cell and that treetop, the sun passing by, the change of light and shadow caused by the clouds, the heat of the sun on my face, and the one thousand different things that I enjoy as an enrichment and clemency.

It is the life of a hermit that I enjoy after having lived a happy, conscious, and eventful life. I have enjoyed it to the fullest, traveling to many beautiful places in the world, together with the best, most loving life partner, my wife, Hilde.

May I use each and every of the remaining days to explore as much spiritual development as possible. For this reason, I thank you for sending me all your loving thoughts, which I will use to keep me conscious.

A noise outside distracted Q for a moment. It was the telltale sound of the guillotine falling down.

"Still writing that legacy of yours?" Werner looked up from the novel he was working on. He must have heard the sound too.

"Yes. You know what? I'm not afraid of dying. Not anymore. It doesn't darken my day nor does it find its way into my dreams."

"That's good to know," Werner said with a smirk.

"I already experienced one death and was quite disappointed to wake up again." Q usually didn't talk about his suicide attempt; in hindsight, it had been a rash and stupid act.

"When my final day arrives, I wish to keep a

dignified posture until my last breath. I won't beg and scream for my life," Werner said.

Q nodded. "We won't give our enemies and the regime the satisfaction of triumphing over our souls."

They remained silent for a few moments before Q spoke again, "I have researched several articles about the death penalty and different execution methods."

Werner shook his head. "So, have you decided on your preferred method yet?"

"You might find this amusing, but I found out that the physical act of dying is the most insignificant part of it. In fact, there are three main methods of execution used."

Werner cast a knowing smile and packed his papers aside. When Q was in discussion mood, it was best to let him talk. "I'm all ears."

"There's the firing squad, which is normally reserved for military personnel or Party members." Q stood in the middle of the cell and counted the methods on his fingers.

"Then there's the guillotine. It's borrowed from the French, and it's an expedient method of separating the head from the body. Compared to the firing squad, the guillotine is a much faster and rather painless method. It's used in our prison.

"And then there's the hanging. This is supposed to be the most painful and dishonoring one. In earlier times, it was mainly reserved for criminals, and they were often hung publicly as a deterrent example for others. It can take several minutes until the death candidate suffocates in agony. This is the method I least prefer."

Werner applauded. "I reckon you also investigated what happens to the bodies?"

"Of course," Q answered with a contented smile. "The bodies of prisoners like us aren't buried. They are taken to the University where they are dissected for medical and scientific discovery."

"Well, isn't that good news? Even after your death, you'll do great things for science!" Werner teased.

Q crumpled a sheet of paper and threw it at Werner. "I should let you continue whatever insignificant things you were doing."

Then he continued writing the letter to his mother. As much as he would have liked to share his discoveries about the different methods of execution with her, he resisted. She would probably appreciate it even less than Werner had.

This letter will show you that I have made my peace with my fate, dear Mother. It is a fate that every human on earth shares with me, as everyone has to die one day.

I have dared to use my freedom of thought as an intellectual person to defy the laws of our cruel government and now have to pay the price for it. But I do it with a raised head and in the reassuring certainty to never have betrayed my conscience like so many others did.

If there is life after death, I can start with a clean conscience and hope to see my beloved wife there.

Sometimes, I believe I am making it too easy for me. Living here in my cell as an intellectual hermit, awaiting the imminent. And sometimes, I believe all of you kind souls are making it too easy for me by thinking of me with such generous and graceful thoughts, sending me letters full of love and not one single word of reproach.

Especially you, my dearest aged but unbowed mother, who is sending me the strength of her thoughts to make me powerful.

Nobody can be praised a happy person looking at death, and yet sometimes, I'm shivering in fear that my current joyful state of mind will suddenly disappear into agony. It might be harder to have to survive and foot the bill for years to come than to go fast and full of illusions.

I wish that all your hopes for peace would come true. I am afraid though that the Gods and powers that be have different plans for the world and most especially for our country. I would have accepted what the Gods handed me and helped rebuild the world. A better world.

A world of peace, mutual respect, and equal opportunities. A world without war, hatred, and humiliation.

You have known me as an impatient person, always on

the lookout to take fate into my own hands, to change the course of events with my own actions.

I believe it was my calling to stem the tide when I set the first foot on this path that has led me to where I am now. Even today, I have no possibility to know if I correctly understood the calling the Gods gave me, or if I misunderstood my purpose of life.

The only thing I could do was to always keep my actions free of lowly and self-serving motives. Everything I did, I was convinced, served a greater good.

Now that I have been caught and my plans sabotaged, I have more than enough time on my hands to meditate in my cell. The meditation has led me to recognize one thing. One thing.

All these struggles in our present time were not meant to be resolved by the action of one individual. Neither were they meant to be resolved from an ambush. No, the Gods have planned this war to end in an open and honest fight.

This war will be fought to the bitter end with sweat, tears, and blood.

Not only the soldiers but also the civilians will have to show endurance and heroic sacrifice. More than anyone is now able to fathom.

Because I had a mission in life, I'm free of regret. The powers that be didn't wish for my intervention. I accept this wish and will leave this world without hard feelings.

Maybe a part of me will remain in this world, maybe I was meant to inspire creative persons to bring out their *very best. Or maybe I was put into this world to procreate, and the important legacy is my two sons.*

Maybe my work in the area of plant protection will one day serve to bring good into the world and feed many hungry people. The more the war took over our daily lives, the more my mind fled into a more peaceful and positive area which I found at the Biological Reich Institute. Even after switching to work for Loewe, I frequently visited my colleagues at the Institute, and we had many fruitful discussions.

The peace of the gardens, the agriculture, and the plants motivated me to work on more productive things than the destructive armaments industry.

Believing that there will be better times after the war where great minds are necessary to rebuild our country and to teach the simple workingman new skills and abilities, I'm sad that I won't be part of that new era, and cannot rush towards a better future with everyone else.

For now, I say, "Solch ein Gewimmel möcht ich sehn ... zum Augenblicke dürft ich sagen: Verweile doch...!" You'll know that part of Faust II by Johann Wolfgang Goethe. So maybe I will still experience my highest moment before those with the spade will come.

I'm glad that my fate has brought you closer to Gunther and his wife as well as to Hilde's wonderful parents.

I also want to reach out my hand to Gunther, hoping he will reach for it, forgetting his dislike for Hilde and without mentioning the past years of estrangement. I wish to reconcile with him before leaving this world.

Despite our differences, Gunther has generously taken over my legal affairs. May he be blessed. How comforting to know that he, too, will help to steer my sons through life, and if so much mercy would be given, helping Hilde if she might stay alive.

I am wishing the best to his sons, especially the youngest who is a flak soldier, with his sweet fifteen years.

Enough blood from our family has flowed in this war and the last one.

Q's hand trembled, and he had to pause. His mind flashed back to a time when he was a young boy, playing with his older brothers, Gunther, Knut, and Albert. They were already in their teens when he was born.

Albert was closest to him in age and mindset. Eleven years older and a gifted mathematician, he helped Q many times with his homework. Q smiled at the memory of how they'd played in their big garden before they moved to Berlin. Q would sit on the swing and Albert would push him until he felt like he was flying into the clouds.

Years later, they discussed scientific problems, and Albert always laughed at his simplistic solutions. But Q admired his brother more than anyone else and vowed to become as brilliant a mind as Albert was when he grew up.

Sadness overwhelmed Q when he traveled through time to the day shortly after his eleventh birthday when Albert left to become a pilot in the Great War. Albert was so full of life, so confident, and looked so handsome in his uniform.

Their mother had waited until he'd walked away before the tears streamed down her face. Q hadn't understood why she cried. Not on that day.

About a year later, they'd received the dreaded telegram. *We are very sorry to inform you that your son Albert Quedlin has been shot down over France.* On that day, Q's life had changed forever. Nothing was as lighthearted as it had been before.

His second oldest brother, Knut, was the black sheep of the family. He preferred to travel instead of holding a steady job. Q had never understood Knut's wanderlust and his need to be anywhere but home.

When Q was twenty-six, his brother had embarked on one of his prolonged excursions. He wanted to travel the entire length of Norway all the way up to the polar circle. Knut was never seen again.

Their mother had clung to the hope for years that her second son would one day show up in her kitchen as he always had. But after seven years, Gunther and Q had insisted she declare him dead. His poor, strong mother.

Soon, only Gunther would be left. The oldest, most responsible of her sons. He and their mother had often butted heads because he was so stubborn in his convictions. For him, everything was black or white, no shades of grey in between. Becoming a lawyer had been inevitable.

Q pursed his lips. Gunther and Hilde had developed a dislike on first sight, and both of them had never been able to get past this first impression. He had to give Gunther great credit to help now when he needed him most. Q hadn't had to ask, Gunther had offered his support to *Herr* Müller without hesitating for one second. He would be a good guardian for Q's sons.

Dusk was falling, and he continued to write...

Now I will say goodbye to you, my beloved mother, because this will probably be the last letter I write to you, except for the day of my execution when I'm allowed to write more than one letter.

From now on, you'll hear about me from Hilde, my beloved wife to whom I owe everything. I dedicate my entire soul and all my rare letters to her.

But I would love to receive letters from you and from everyone who is able and willing to write me. They are the highlights of my reclusive life. There's no need to refer back to this letter in your answers, we do not want to bother the censors with insignificant details.

Your letters keep me in a good mood. News from the family and especially from my dear children keeps me connected to my former world, that's now only your world. It keeps the solitude away from my heart. It would be wonderful if the family could take turns in writing, this way not all the burden falls upon you, my beloved mother.

I will never forget our shared memories. Most of the past I see with a photographic memory. You at the end station of the tram line 44 where you waited for me to return from school. And your apartment. I can even smell the herb tea you used to brew when I visited. This way I never feel alone in my isolation, and every letter from the outside brings life to those pictures in my mind.

Please give my best greetings to everyone. With Annie Klein, you do not talk anymore? Such a pity because she is such a good soul, sacrificing, with a good heart, but little education.

One note to everyone: please don't put money in the letters, only stamps.

Today is Friday, and according to my observations, they don't come to fetch on weekends, so I'll most probably still be alive when you receive this letter on Monday, June 21.

Mid-summer.

On December 20 I almost died, and now, half a year later I'm still here. And have we not deepened our bond through this letter?

Goodbye. Farewell. Thank you for everything you gave me, including the healthy constitution which I hope my children have inherited.

We are now connected spiritually.

Your son, Wilhelm

It was almost midnight, and the dusk was giving way to a few short hours of darkness. Q stared at the paper until the letters blurred. There was so much more he wanted to tell his mother, but this would be his last letter to her. Honest person that she was, she had made it clear in no uncertain words that she refused to receive secret messages from him.

Chapter 34

Hilde was in a quandary. She'd been told a few minutes ago, that on July fifteenth, she would once again be allowed a visit from her sons. But she had to choose one child.

"Margit, what shall I do?" she asked her cellmate.

"That's a difficult question, indeed." Margit put a hand to her chin and wrinkled her forehead. "Which one do you want to see more urgently?"

"Of course, both of them," Hilde sighed. "The last time Volker visited was three months ago, but I haven't seen Peter since I was arrested...and I would love to see how he can walk...and talk. Hear him speak so many words with his little voice."

"Then take Peter," Margit suggested.

"I don't know. Do you think he still remembers me? He was barely nine months old when I had to leave him with Mother Annie." Hilde stood and paced the room. She looked out the small window to the trees in full blossom, and then she turned around to glance at Margit. "What if he doesn't recognize me? What if he has no idea who that strange woman is? Wouldn't that disturb his little mind?"

"Hmm, I don't think so, but then take Volker," Margit said.

"I really want to see Peter..."

"Perhaps you shouldn't think what you want, but what is best for your children," Margit suggested in an attempt to help Hilde take the emotions out of this decision.

"You're probably right...Peter doesn't even know what a mother is. If he sees me here, how strange will that be for him? It wouldn't mean anything to him." Hilde nodded. "It's more important that Volker comes to visit. I want him to recognize me as his mother if I ever get out of here."

"He does have pictures of you," Margit argued.

"Yes, but it's not the same. Maybe he won't forget me if he sees me at least once in a while. He's such an intelligent boy." Hilde smiled at the memories invading her mind. "If Emma keeps telling him about his mother, and if I hopefully get out of here one day, then I'm not just a strange aunt he's never met before."

"Won't the trip to Berlin be too strenuous for him?" Margit asked.

"No. We took him on trips when he was much smaller, and he has always liked it. He has a healthy constitution and is curious enough to enjoy new surroundings."

"Don't you think he might be disturbed? If he's as

intelligent as you say, he'll find out that this is not a hospital, but a prison."

"Perhaps." Hilde wrinkled her nose as she thought for a few moments before she continued to speak. "Even if he'll be slightly deranged by the visit, if you were in my situation, wouldn't you want to see him?"

"Of course I would. So, take Volker."

"I will. And if I'm not allowed to live, then he will at least have a memory of his mother." Tears pooled in Hilde's eyes.

Three more weeks and she would wrap her arms around her beloved son again.

***

A few days later, a letter from Q arrived. She tore it open and devoured his words.

My beloved Hilde,

Oh, how I loved receiving your last letter and that precious picture of our little boys. Thank you from the bottom of my heart. I admit, I cried when I saw how much they both have grown, but I know that they are safe and being cared for...that is all I could ask for.

As to your question about packages from Annie. Yes, she does send me one every month, and I'm very grateful for her continued support. It always contains much needed food and stamps (we are not allowed to have money, but can use the stamps to buy certain things).

Despite me not being allowed to receive visitors, your kind mother has managed to change Kriminalkommissar Becker's mind and came to visit me.

Hilde stared at the paper. Mother Annie had visited Q? How? Or better: Why? She continued to read with curiosity.

I was immensely grateful and happy about her visit, but I'm afraid she didn't feel the same joy at the results of our discussion. Your self-sacrificing mother had wished to attain custody over our two boys, but in line with what you and I have talked earlier, I had to refuse her wish. Instead, I told her that my brother Gunther, who is well versed in all legal affairs, is our preferred guardian for the children.

Hilde giggled loud enough to attract Margit's attention, who shot her a questioning glance.

"It's just Q. He's so funny," Hilde explained and imagined how Q and her mother had been sitting in the visiting room. Both of them staring at each other, and her mother growing exasperated as she grasped that she wouldn't get her way with Q. It had been like that with them for years. Q had always been polite and kind to Annie, but he'd never succumbed to her charms like everyone else did. Apparently even *Kriminalkommissar* Becker.

Hilde put the letter to her nose, Q's smell still lingering on the paper, and started to read again.

I have received several letters from Emma, and even one from your sister Sophie. Please give them my heartfelt thanks if you have the opportunity to do so.

Not a day goes by that I don't regret the circumstances that led to your imprisonment. Please forgive me! If there were a way I could spare you what lies ahead, I would do so…even with my own life. My love, I do not want to raise your spirits in vain, but there might be hope for you.

Hilde paused and shook her head. She bore Q no ill will and wasn't upset with him. She had supported his decisions and actions out of free will. It would have been easy to walk away and save herself had she wished to.

Q had even suggested abandoning her and the children after a feigned fight to keep them safe. But she had objected.

She turned her attention back to her husband's letter.

I am in good health and have been generously allowed to continue my scientific work. It is such a relief for my mind to meditate and to ponder on the solution of scientific problems. You know me well enough to understand how I tend to get absorbed in my work. It fills endless hours and time flies by. As peculiar as it sounds, I am quite happy with my current situation. The only thing I wish for is to have you by my side.

Hilde felt a twinge of jealousy. Q was working and had something to occupy his day while she had nothing to do. She would ask Emma to send her Sophie's old school books. Then she could keep her mind occupied with practicing French or learning history.

Instinctively, she grabbed the Japer pendant around her neck that Q's mother had given her. The stone warmed quickly to the touch of her hand and never failed to give her confidence.

Her thoughts wandered to Ingrid, and a surge of empathy filled her soul. Q would be the third of her four sons to die. A fate no mother should have to endure. Hilde decided to ask for permission to write an extra letter next month. That letter would go to Ingrid.

Then she turned back to Q's letter, reading the many spoonerisms he wrote for her. Soon enough she was holding her stomach from laughing.

"What are you giggling about over there?" Margit asked.

"Q's letter. He wrote a bunch of spoonerisms," Hilde answered and started to recite, but was interrupted by a guard opening their cell door.

"Leisure time," she announced and sent them

down to the courtyard for their daily walk.

"Take the letter with you and read those spoonerisms to us," Margit urged her.

Hilde nodded and folded the letter into her pocket as they joined the other prisoners in the courtyard. Hilde recited a few of the verses, and attracted by Margit's and Hilde's giggles, several other inmates and even some guards gathered around to listen.

"Let's see if you can guess what the words should have been? Drear fiend." Hilde glanced around expectantly as the women repeated the words.

One of them grinned and called out, "Dear friend."

"That's it. Now, try this one. I hissed my mystery lectures."

Margit beamed, "That one is easy. I missed my history lectures."

"Good. One more. You have a nosey little crook there." Hilde watched as the women mouthed the words to themselves.

Finally, one of the guards spoke up, "You have a cozy little nook there."

"Precisely," Hilde said.

Margit touched her arm. "Thank you for sharing those with us." She looked around at the gathered group and sighed, "We don't laugh enough around here."

Chapter 35

Q had received non-committal indications from Göring that Hilde's plea for clemency would be looked upon favorably, but nothing official. He was drip-feeding the *Kriegsmarine*, the German navy with small, albeit unimportant improvements for the acoustic torpedoes. By doing so, he wouldn't give away his discoveries before Hilde's sentence was revoked, while nobody could accuse him of a lack of cooperation.

One day in July, Q's lawyer visited with news to share.

"I spoke with Erhard Tohmfor's wife to give my condolences for her husband's death," *Herr* Müller said.

A knot tied up Q's throat. His good friend was dead. Gone forever. One of the kindest, must upright men he'd known.

"How is she?" Q asked when he regained control over his voice.

"*Frau* Tohmfor is fine as the case may be. She was arrested, but the Gestapo released her after a short time. I had hoped she could give me information that would be helpful with your appeal."

"I don't want to appeal. I've been rightly accused of treason, and I accept the power of the authorities to punish me for breaking their law. My mission in life, one I freely took upon myself, was to bring the current government down."

"There is still a chance–" *Herr* Müller pleaded.

"No." Q shook his head. "I would rather you spend your time and my money to receive a milder sentence for my wife. My case is lost."

Herr Müller nodded although he clearly didn't agree. "As you wish."

"I do have a request for you, though," Q said.

"Go on." *Herr* Müller glanced at his watch. "We have a few more minutes left."

"Could you contact a dear friend of mine, Leopold Stieber, and ask him if he'd be willing to help care for my children once I'm not on this earth anymore."

The lawyer agreed, and Q gave him Leopold's address. When it was time to bid goodbye, *Herr* Müller handed him an issue of the Nazi propaganda newspaper *Völkischer Beobachter*. "You might be interested in the news."

"Thank you, I'm sure this reading material will lift my spirits," Q said with a sarcastic tone.

"It might, given that you are waiting for this war to be over. The four-year anniversary of the declaration of war from England is nearing. As far as

I'm concerned, there's no person in this country who isn't waiting for the end," *Herr* Müller said and prepared to leave. "Someone contacted me a few days ago. The man wouldn't reveal his name, but insisted I let you know he was safe."

Q nodded thoughtfully. The lawyer didn't say another word but proceeded to hug Q, which was unusual to say the least. "I'll be back in a few weeks."

"Have a nice day," Q answered, trying to find a reason for *Herr* Müller's strange behavior.

The guard searched the newspaper for hidden messages and then led him back to his cell. Absent-mindedly, Q tossed the newspaper on the table and dug his hands into his pockets, where his fingers touched a piece of paper that hadn't been there before.

Q plopped onto the bunk bed and unfolded it.

Please destroy this letter immediately.

After your arrest and the arrest of E, I tried to get in touch with persons I knew by name. In vain. Everything was cut off. I didn't dare ask around, for the constant terror to be discovered myself.

I'm safe and continue to work as always, although the situation became more critical for me every day. But now things have calmed down, and I continue with our work.

It is only because of your and E's pertinacity that I am still alive. My life is indebted to you for never mentioning my name. And I admire you for acting ruthlessly against yourself. Steadfast and strong. You were the brilliant mind and E was the natural born leader who knew like no other to lead us the correct way.

A way that I will continue to honor, despite the additional difficulties. I lack the connections you and E had, but that doesn't bother me. Rest assured that I will continue to work for our cause with unwavering effort, maybe even with more enthusiasm than before.

I learned about E's unfortunate end several days ago, and the fact that this inhuman regime has annihilated one of the best persons I've known gives me strength to carry on every day.

During a recent air raid, I had to hear that 'we have to thank the pig Q for those attacks from our enemies.'

You can't imagine how much I wait for the day of the planned upheaval.

X

The letter was typewritten, but there was no mistaking that Martin was the sender.

Q smiled and took solace in the fact that he'd at least been able to save one of his friends. He tore the paper into tiny pieces and swallowed them. Martin had taken a big – and useless – risk writing this letter, but nevertheless, it was nice to know he continued to sabotage the military production at Loewe.

Maybe there was hope for Germany.

The next day, news about the war reached the prisoners. During their leisure time in the courtyard, nervous whispers shared the developments of the past week.

"The Red Army has launched a devastating attack on our Wehrmacht in Kursk," one of the guards said with an unusually serene face. "Both my brother and my cousin are in the 4th Panzer Army. I'm afraid they won't return home."

One of the Russian prisoners grinned and raised his hands, seemingly asking for God's help to defeat the Germans.

"It doesn't look good for Hitler," another prisoner added, "the British, Canadian, and American troops have invaded Sicily. There are rumors they have conquered all major ports in Sicily."

Q's memory returned to his honeymoon. *Licata, Gela, Pachino, Avola, Noto, Pozzallo, Scoglitti, Ispica, Rosolini,* and Syracuse. It seemed like centuries ago that he and Hilde had visited the ancient Sicilian ports. Back in 1937, Sicily had been peaceful, calm, and hospitable. They'd even joked about staying there forever and becoming wine farmers.

"I wonder how much longer Mussolini will resist the combined forces of the Western Allies," Q murmured.

"If the Italian's can't help themselves, we'll go and do it for them," one of the guards said.

Q shook his head. "The *Wehrmacht* is bleeding out. Where should the replacements for the many fallen soldiers come from? Even my sixteen-year-old nephew has been drafted to handle flak."

"Pah, that's black propaganda from the enemy, our losses are minimal," the guard responded.

But Q believed otherwise. Before being arrested, he'd listened daily to foreign radio stations and their numbers always differed widely from those presented by the propaganda ministry.

"One day, you will remember my words. In a year from now, Hitler and his Reich of a Thousand Years will be nothing but rubble. People like you will be the ones to shoulder the burden to rebuild our country from the ashes. The suffering will be tremendous. Much worse than anything we experience now."

Chapter 36

Hilde was lying on her bed, wallowing in self-pity. Volker was sick and hadn't been able to travel to Berlin.

"If I can't see Volker, I won't go to see my mother either," she whined.

"That's plain stupid," Margit told her. "Any visitor is better than moping around in here. I'm sure you will enjoy seeing your mother."

"I won't. I want to see my son! My son!"

In the end, Hilde dragged herself to the visiting room, but only because Margit insisted. And maybe because she was the tiniest bit curious what news her mother would bring from the lawyer.

As she entered the visiting room, she was surprised to find two people waiting for her. It took a few moments before she recognized her half-brother, Klaus. He'd grown and towered over her by at least a head. His shoulders had broadened, and his face had lost the chubby childlike look.

"You've grown so tall." Hilde hugged her brother.

"I'm not a boy anymore," he reminded her with the pride of a teenager who wanted to be a man, "I'm a soldier now. A *Luftwaffenhelfer*."

Hilde nodded and shook her mother's hand. "A soldier at fifteen? That's awful."

"I turned sixteen several weeks ago," he protested and did his best to stand taller.

After exchanging some pleasantries, Hilde asked the question preying on her mind. "Do you have news from *Herr* Müller, Mother?"

"Indeed. *Herr* Müller has telephoned me to announce that your clemency appeal has been filed. It will be brought to the attention of the *Führer* himself to decide upon. *Herr* Müller is confident that the *Führer* will give a positive answer."

Hilde shrugged her shoulders. She should be elated but wasn't.

"That doesn't seem to make you happy," Annie said.

"I'm trying not to get my hopes up too much, and I can't imagine living without my Q."

Annie shook her head. "How can you say that? He is responsible for all of this."

"Mother, I don't expect you to understand this, but only now after going through these bad times can I really appreciate how good a man Q is. He's the love of my life, never more so than now."

"How is he still alive?" Klaus asked. "I understood they have executed all traitors from that Schulze-Boysen group."

Hilde squeezed his arm at the mention of the execution rooms. "Q is working scientifically again, and the government is hoping to gain useful research from him. That is the only reason he is still alive. They'll hold him as a prisoner as long as he's useful to them and then..."

"And you still tell me he's such a good man? He's betraying his own faulty ideals and now works for the government he hated so much? To buy himself time? What about you? Why doesn't he offer his work in exchange for your release?" Annie talked herself into a rage.

"Mother, there's nothing left for me out there, and the only reason I want to live is for the sake of my boys." It was hard to explain, but every day she felt a greater distance between her and the outside world. She didn't belong anymore, and she didn't know if she could return to a normal life after what she'd gone through.

One moment she accepted her fate, and the next one, she was paralyzed by terror and wanted to scream, *Let me live! I want to live!*

"Your boys need their mother." Annie averted her eyes. "You will be with them, perhaps even for your birthday in five weeks."

"I'm not so sure, Mother. If Germany loses the war, they will kill all of us before the end."

"Our *Führer* won't allow that to happen. We will win this war," Klaus said with youthful enthusiasm.

The Nazi propaganda had worked perfectly on her brother.

Annie nodded. "There, you hear it. And in the unlikely case our enemies should win, I'm positive you will have been released already. The Nazis aren't barbarians. Your plea for clemency will be approved."

Hilde put a hand over her heart, hoping her mother was right. But even if she was spared, Q didn't have the slightest reason to expect mercy. During his interrogations and his trial, and even now in his letters to her, he openly defied the Nazi ideology, calling it one of the worst evils in the world. The eighth deadly sin.

He had made it too clear that he was on the side of our enemies, they wouldn't give him the satisfaction of having been right. His unwavering opposition hadn't made things easier for her either. The judge believed she had the same convictions as her husband. While that was true, she'd been careful to never admit it.

Would she really have to die because of those two letters she wrote for him?

As for Q, if the Allies won and found out he was assisting the Reich, they would be less lenient with him and might order his death themselves. I pity him.

Her mother interrupted her thoughts as she stepped closer, looping her arm with Hilde's before dropping something into her daughter's pocket.

"What's that?" Hilde mouthed.

"Tranquilizers," Annie whispered into her ear. "Take them in case...you know."

Chapter 37

Q had been waiting to hear back from *Herr* Müller with news from Leopold. In the event that both he and Hilde were executed, he wanted to secure as much support from Leopold for their two sons as possible. Leopold was a well-connected factory owner, jovial, honest and with high moral standards.

They had been friends since high school, and Q knew that Leopold had lost his parents at an early age and had later been adopted. He understood from firsthand experience how much orphaned children required moral support from different sources.

The lawyer had asked to meet with Q in the open courtyard, where it was harder for the guard to eavesdrop. The request was granted, and Q joined him, the pair walking slowly around the perimeter as they spoke.

"Did you find Leopold?" Q asked quietly, keeping his eyes straight ahead.

"Yes and no. He was captured and charged with high treason."

Q almost lost his composure, but he remained strong and asked, "What did he do?"

"You really want to make me believe you had no idea he was working in the resistance? They accused him of being a part of the Red Orchestra network." *Herr* Müller pierced Q with his eyes.

"I...had no idea," Q stammered. "I...he...he never told me."

"Well, your friend was discharged and found not guilty."

"They acquitted him?" Q asked louder than intended, relief flooding his system.

Herr Müller nodded and then moved his eyes to the side to indicate the growing interest from the guards. Both he and Q started walking again.

"He must have powerful connections, but apparently not powerful enough. They didn't release him into freedom but rather transferred to the concentration camp Sachsenhausen."

"After finding him not guilty?" Q asked incredulously.

"Yes. Unfortunately, the instrument of protective custody can be used against anyone at any time. I found out that he's doing forced labor in an industrial complex. The owner can't speak highly enough of your friend."

Q processed the news in silence, until the lawyer spoke again, "What do you know about Stieber's parents?"

"He became an orphan early on and was later

adopted. His parents are nice people, I've met them several times." Q wondered why the lawyer wanted to know about Leopold's parents.

"Did you know they are Romani?"

"Romani?" Q hissed. "I had no idea." What else did he not know about his friend?

"They changed their last name shortly after they adopted Leopold and moved to Berlin to start with a clean slate. I'm not certain whether he knew or not when he was a child. But he definitely knew after 1939 when his father died, and his mother went into hiding. She might be the reason why he joined the Resistance."

Q didn't answer. A sick feeling of betrayal spread across his body. He and Leopold had known each other for more than twenty years, had even been good friends, and yet his friend had never seen fit to tell him the truth. Not about his parents. Not about his opposition to the government.

It's not like I was completely honest with him either. Q realized that both of them had kept secrets they didn't want anyone else to know. He chuckled at the irony. *It's funny. We've been friends for more than half of our lives, and yet we never knew the other one was working for the same cause.*

The lawyer remained quiet as well, and after a while, the tension became unbearable.

"You have other news," Q stated matter-of-factly.

"Yes. Shall we find a place to sit?"

"No. Just tell me." Q increased his pace to get away from the prying ears of the guards.

"Very well. Hitler and Goebbels are still very indignant about your assassination plan."

Q drew a breath and clasped his hands together. "That doesn't sound like it bodes well for me."

"It doesn't. I received word that they are planning to publicly hang you in front of the Loewe factory."

The blood froze in his veins. *They want to make an example of me.*

Chapter 38

Hilde sat in her cell, fingering the tranquilizers her mother had given her. Despite the aggravating circumstances, Annie's gesture moved her to tears. It probably was the nicest thing anyone had done for her in a while.

She vowed to work on a better relationship with her mother if she ever returned to freedom.

Several days later, Hilde seized the opportunity to buy paper for a secret message to her stepmother. Volker hadn't been able to travel for the scheduled visit, but she could at least write him.

Dear Mother Emma,

You cannot mention this letter because it is not an official one. Send me in your answer with the second sentence starting with "yes my dear Hilde." This will be my clue that you received the letter.

My sincerest thanks for your last letter and for the nice pictures. You can't imagine my joy! Little Peter looks so cute standing beside his bigger brother, and I can see how he crumples his nose. It warms my heart. This is the first picture where you and dad are photographed as well. Now

I have all four of you here with me in my prison cell.

I yearn to see my children again and am waiting for permission to at least see Volker. Mother Annie has promised me to ask, but we must wait until she comes back from her trip to the Baltic Sea.

As soon as I have held my dear little Volker in my arms again, I will be patient until I can see you and Daddy again. I hope that I will still be alive in half a year and maybe, just maybe, the war will be over by then. Wouldn't that be a joyous day?

Since yesterday, I am more confident because I have heard, already for the second time, that women are not executed anymore. I have also heard about three women who we thought had been killed, but no, they are still alive.

Following the advice of my lawyer, I have written an addition to my plea for clemency, and now wish to hope again. Hope for a little bit of life. I do not want to live for myself because I am not suitable for this world anymore. It is for the sake of my children that I hope.

At least I know that my children are in the very best hands with you, and of course, you shall decide fully about them. If I do not stay alive, the children can go and live with Q's cousin Fanny in America after the war. They would have a good life overseas. And you wouldn't have the burden of raising two more children now that your own are grown up. Please do not worry about the future.

How is your health? You never write about yourself, and you have all the work with the children. What about your legs and your heart, and can you sleep enough? Do you often have alarm?

I always smile when you write me about them, how Daddy takes them with him to his clients and what they like. Now in these warm summer days, I think even more about my sons. How we bathed in the lake. Had a picnic on the grass. We had plans to take them to the lake or the Baltic Sea this summer, if this horrible fate hadn't come over us.

Regarding your concern about sending Volker to Mother Annie, I don't think it will be bad for him, and it will bring you some relief. He is so much smarter than I was when I first came to you so many years ago.

Mother Annie will spoil him, that is for sure. But he'll be with her just a few days, and once he's back with you, he will surely accept that, at your place, he has to behave.

I pray it will be the last time he comes to visit me here. My lawyer is confident that my plea for clemency will be approved. Then they will take me to another place. A normal prison is so much better than here, where everyone is waiting for the worst.

And if God is with us, then this war will soon be over, and we can all be together again. Therefore, please think of this visit as the last one. Who knows how everything will look after another six months.

Please receive my sincerest thanks for everything you're doing for me. The cookies were delicious. You cannot imagine how bad the food is here. And if you don't receive food from outside, then it is a horrible hunger. They have reduced our rations twice since I'm here. Apparently, they think prisoners can subsist on love and air alone...and there's not much love in here.

Thank you so much for the books, they are the biggest help because I'm always bored.

And give both my sons a big kiss from me. Don't let them ever forget about their mother. I'm not forgetting them either. On the contrary, I think of them every waking minute of the day and dream of them at night. I will love them until my last breath and beyond.

Love,

Hilde

She folded the two sheets of paper and squeezed them into an envelope, sealing it. Now she would have to wait until one of the nice guards was on duty and pay her to deliver the letter to the next mail office.

Hilde hoped to have the verdict on her pleas for clemency by the time she received Emma's answer. Then she could – with God's help – send her stepmother positive news.

Chapter 39

Q received a letter from his mother and read it for the umpteenth time.

My dear Wilhelm,

I want to thank you so much for your long and detailed letter. I have read it several times, and it has given me a clearer picture of your state of mind and your fate.

But I also must tell you that my soul is sick after reading it. My moods are swinging up and down in a turbulent, even violent manner.

While I will always love you and send you strengthening thoughts, I wish you would show remorse for the great guilt you've loaded upon yourself.

Both Gunther and I telegraphed Kriminalkommissar Becker and asked for permission to visit you. Denied.

Q looked up to where Werner sat at the table. "Becker denied my poor mother permission to visit again. She must be out of her mind," Q complained.

"You mustn't let despair take over." Werner tried to calm him down.

"With her seventy-seven years and frail health, she begged him to see me one last time. And that cruel son of a bitch denied her request." Q sighed, burying his head in his hands.

"You must hold out hope that *Kriminalkommissar* Becker will relent sometime soon."

"Sometime soon?" Q asked him, a hint of sarcasm in his voice. "How much time do I, do you, have left? Every day can be the last one."

Werner shook his head. "None of us knows that. We've been here much longer than most of the other prisoners."

"Why? Why hasn't my sentence been enforced yet?" Q surged to his feet and paced the tiny space.

"I don't know the answer to that question. No one in this prison knows the answer. Those things are decided higher up the ranks."

"Nobody tells me or my family. We can only speculate. It might be because I'm sharing my research with the government. They might wait and see if they can get anything useful out of me."

"That is a good thing, correct?" Werner asked.

"Yes and no." Q ran a hand through his tousled hair. Since he was in prison, he didn't wear it short anymore, and his curls gave him an Afro hairstyle. "Gunther visited Becker and asked what my chances were in case they petitioned for mercy on my behalf."

"What was his answer?"

Instead of a response, Q read from the letter:

Kriminalkommissar Becker told your brother that, of course, every family is free to petition for mercy. Then Gunther contacted your public defendant but received the same answer.

Werner scoffed. "What else would they say? Those Nazis have their mind made up, there's no backing up."

"At least the public defendant promised to discuss the subject with the responsible people at the *Reichskriegsgericht.*"

"You know that he probably won't follow through with his promise?"

"Yes, I know that." Q nodded and silence settled in the cell.

After reading his mother's letter again, Q said, "I will ask her not to file a plea of mercy."

Werner's head snapped around. "Why not?"

"It would be ineffectual."

"You can't give up hope. You have to be strong and believe that somehow this situation will right itself."

"I'm not giving up, but my spirit is already beyond the confines of this world. I'm not afraid of the end anymore. What I'm afraid of is changing my sentence to lifelong imprisonment. I don't want to put that burden on anyone. I have no place and no use in this world any longer."

"That is not true," Werner insisted.

"It is. And my mother will understand. Maybe she'll even be proud of me. One day," Q said, hoping that one day in the future his mother would come to understand why he had chosen to break the laws and work on the demise of this government.

"The end is near, my friend," Werner said. "The Russians are pushing the *Wehrmacht* farther West every day."

Q nodded, and the men lapsed into silence, leaving Q to think of the past.

It all started with the re-militarization after the Great War. Hitler explained it was to rectify the treaty of Versailles. And nothing would have happened if he'd stopped there. But the very moment he started his aggression on his former ally, Russia, things went down the drain.

Even without opening the Eastern front and going to war with Russia, it was a very risky undertaking to fight against the Allies.

All those sacrifices in vain again. Soldiers dying for nothing.

Some countries like Sweden and Switzerland knew that those who came out of any war the happiest was the one who never went in.

Chapter 40

Time was slipping away, and as July ended and headed into August, the news coming from the outside was terror-filled for Hilde. On July twenty-fifth, the Allies had begun daily raids on Hamburg in an operation called Gomorrha. Every day the death toll rose, quickly approaching thirty thousand.

Hilde fretted and cried, and Margit had given up trying to console her until a letter from Emma arrived.

Dearest Hilde,

You have probably heard about the horrible bombings over Hamburg. The boys and I left the city immediately after the government advised all citizens to evacuate. We are now with my cousin who lives in the countryside.

Your father and Sophie remained behind because they are needed in the war effort.

I will send you a longer letter as soon as I find the time,

Your mother, Emma

Hilde gave a long sigh. "Margit, good news!

Emma and my sons are safe in the countryside."

"See, I told you they would be fine." Margit beamed as she climbed down from the top bunk.

"I'm so thankful she took them away from Hamburg, but how hard must it be for my father and Sophie to be alone in these hard times? She should reunite with them as soon as possible. Who is more important, her husband and daughter or her grandsons?"

"That question can only be answered by higher powers than we are," Margit answered.

"Bloody Hitler! Without him and his stupid war, none of us would be suffering now," Hilde exclaimed.

"Shush." Margit placed a finger over her lips. "Be careful, you never know who is listening."

Hilde rolled her eyes. "I'm already sentenced to death, remember? There's no need to be careful anymore."

Both women burst into a fit of giggles at the irony of the situation. When Hilde was able to breathe again, she said, "Anyway, Emma should be with her family. It is important during these times."

Margit frowned. "I disagree. I wouldn't want to be with my Nazi family."

Hilde looked at her friend with empathy. *If you didn't have a family you loved, what was worth living in your life?* "Maybe I should ask Emma not to travel with Volker to Berlin, although I really, really want to see him."

"Berlin is a horrible place right now with the constant shelling and firebombs. The Blonde Angel told me that the government might order an evacuation of the city soon."

"I bet they don't extend that to the prisoners." Hilde scoffed.

"Probably not. So far, the Propaganda Ministry has asked all non-working women and children to evacuate Berlin on a voluntary basis."

"What would the guards say if we volunteered to leave the city?" Hilde giggled.

Margit joined her giggles, and for a short moment, they forgot the reality, but then Hilde sobered. "I wonder if Q's mother has left the city. The last time she wrote me a letter, she told me that half of her one-bedroom apartment had been seized to house others whose living quarters had been bombed."

"I can't imagine living in such close quarters with people you don't know." Margit sighed theatrically, and Hilde burst into another fit of laughter.

"You mean like you and I do?" she asked.

Margit furrowed her brows as if she had to think about the situation. Then she slowly nodded her head. "That's different, though. Anyhow, things in Berlin are bad, and I believe they're only going to get worse."

***

A few days later, Hilde received a letter stamped with the Imperial Eagle carrying the Swastika.

"Oh my God, Margit, it's from the *Reichskriegsgericht*," Hilde said and held the letter in her trembling fingers. "I can't open it."

"Shall I help you?" Margit asked, trying to snatch the envelope from Hilde's hands.

"No. Don't you dare." Hilde sat down on her bed and fumbled the letter from the court open.

In big red letters, the word *Abgelehnt* stared at her, and her eyes filled with tears. The sheet of paper sailed to the floor, where Margit gathered it and read it.

"Oh Hilde, I'm so sorry. Your appeal for clemency appeal has been denied. By Hitler himself. There's no explanation as to why. It just says this decision is final." Margit sat down beside Hilde and wrapped her in her arms, where she cried like a baby.

"It's dated July 21, 1943," Hilde whispered between sobs. "It's taken them more than a week to notify me."

Margit held Hilde for a long time without uttering a word. She knew nothing could console her friend, whose hopes for a future had been shattered with one single word. *Abgelehnt.*

***

Three days later, two guards entered their cell, and Hilde jumped with terror. *They have come for me.*

"Gather your things," one of them said, pointing at Margit, "you are released."

"I'm released?" Margit almost fell from the upper bunk bed in her haste to get out of the cell before the guards changed their mind.

"Yes. Hurry."

"I'm getting out," Margit whispered as she hastily grabbed her few possessions. On her way out, she hugged Hilde tightly. "Don't give up hope. Remember that the Blonde Angel said that women aren't executed anymore."

"Thank you for being such a good friend. Live a good life." Hilde clung to her friend, sadness sweeping over her. How would she stay sane in here without Margit's cheerful companionship?

The guard cleared her throat.

Hilde knew Margit's father had arranged for her release because she'd finally agreed to put on a good face and fake remorse. She'd apologized to him for the error of her ways even while she'd discussed with her fellow prisoners how to best work in the underground to oppose the regime and help those less fortunate than she was.

"I need to leave," Margit whispered and turned

around. In the door, she squared her shoulders and walked out of the cell, out of the prison.

Freedom was hers once more.

At least one of them might survive.

Chapter 41

Q looked up from his research with surprise. *Pfarrer* Bernau stood in front of the small table. If Q wasn't mistaken, his weekly visit wasn't due for another two days.

"What brings you here, *Pfarrer*?" Q asked.

"I'm afraid nothing good. My colleague at your wife's prison has told me that her clemency appeal was denied."

Q slumped into his chair and buried his face in his palms. "This is all my fault."

"You must stop blaming yourself. It is not your fault, and you know this." The priest tried to console him, but Q wouldn't listen.

"Her birthday is three weeks from now. She'll turn thirty-one, and I won't be with her." It took all his self-control not to break down into tears.

The priest laid a hand on his shoulder. "Your wife knows your spirit is with her."

"It's not the same." Q's voice broke, and he had to breathe several times to gain control again. "If I had known what would happen...that I would be the reason for Hilde's condemnation...that I would kill the one person in this world I love the most...I would have done things differently."

"You wouldn't have fought against the Nazis?"

Q shook his head and tried to find the right words. "No. Of course I would still have pursued this mission, but I would have taken greater measures to protect her. Leave her. Disappear." He paused and then questioned his last statement. "I wonder what would have been worse...breaking her heart or ending her life?"

"None of us knows what the future will hold, and we have to put our faith in God that He knows where to put us on this earth," *Pfarrer* Bernau said with a solemn face.

"I was so careful and have successfully kept secret the extent to which I despise the Nazis. My little talk against the National Socialism here and there was nothing compared to what I really feel. But that I would destroy my most loyal friends..." Q shook his head. "I should have stopped all contacts with fellow scientists and engineers."

"Why them?" the priest wondered.

"There's not an engineer out there who doesn't know some military secrets. How do you think it was so easy for me to gather intelligence? Was it possible for me to anticipate this?" Q's chest fell with despair, and he looked at *Pfarrer* Bernau as if he could, by some miracle, redeem him from his guilt.

"We will never know this. God's ways are inscrutable."

"But these are the questions that weigh heavily on my conscience. And I'm afraid for everyone who is truly innocent even in the sense of the court. Whose only mistake has been to know me. Maybe even the good director of the Biological Reichs Institute, who let me work for the institution?" Q grew more desperate by the minute.

"You cannot burden yourself with guilt for the injustices the current regime commits. It is not your fault, and rest assured that every person has to step in front of the Last Judgment when his time has come."

"If only the earthly court would let me testify before my death, then I would energetically and without a shadow of a doubt tell them that nobody has helped me except for my good friend and boss at Loewe, Erhard. Then my life would still be useful if I could rescue someone else with my testimony."

"What makes you think the court would believe you this time? Haven't the judges shown time and again that truth does not matter to them?" the priest asked and folded his hands.

"Erhard, my conscious and active helper is already dead. My wife will undoubtedly follow his path," Q growled like a wounded animal.

"That, we do not know. Just because her appeal for clemency has been denied doesn't mean she'll be executed. I haven't had to accompany a woman in a long time."

Q closed his eyes, trying to conjure up pictures of happier times. Times when he and Hilde had been together. Happy.

Her unconstrained laughter had mesmerized him before he'd even seen her for the first time. But that was history now. Q had no idea how long he'd indulged in reminiscences when the sound of someone clearing his throat brought him back to the present.

"*Pfarrer* Bernau, while I wished to dedicate my life to the pursuit of spiritual, cultural, and intellectual development, I had to fulfill the mundane necessity of earning money."

The priest smiled. "I know very well that feeling."

"At the same time, I decided early in my career to find ways to strengthen my Russian friends and weaken their enemies."

"If we can believe the news coming from the East, Stalin is betraying the ideals that made him great." *Pfarrer* Bernau furrowed his brows. "But I still tend to believe he's the lesser of two evils. How is your experience with the Russians?"

"They were always respectful and polite. My contacts never once urged me to change my profession and pursue a career that might be of more value for them. They respected the individual, me, which is a very high good."

"You liked these agents?"

Q nodded. "I did. The agents I met were fine people I simply had no choice but to like. We shared the same ideals and worked together for a good cause..." Q grew quiet and thought of the double agent who betrayed him. Even after eight months, this vicious deed stabbed at his heart. He had trusted this man – with his life. And now, not only would he pay, but so many others would too.

Chapter 42

On the morning of August 5, 1943, Hilde was transferred to Plötzensee. This could only mean one thing: her time on this earth had come to an end.

"You can write as many goodbye letters as you wish," the guard said not unkindly as he gave her paper and pen. Then he left the cell and bolted the door.

Hilde stared at the door and then down at the paper. So many times she'd been afraid of this exact moment, but now that it had come, she was calm, even numb.

She sighed and fingered the tranquilizers her mother Annie had given her. She would use them later, after writing her letters. Because for those she needed a clear and sharp mind.

Her relationship with her mother had been complicated, but with the Grim Reaper waiting for Hilde, none of their quarrels mattered anymore. Despite all her shortcomings, Annie loved her daughter and had shown that she cared. It was time to make peace.

My *beloved mother,*

It is the most terrible of all things that I have to give you this heartache. I have a few hours left and am calm and composed.

Please take solace in my sweet little boys, and you also have your son. If Klaus survives this cruel war, I'm sure he will bring you only joy. My best wishes for him. He should not get involved in politics, let him take on a harmless profession like a musician or something similar.

What else shall I say? I cannot allow myself to become too soft in theses hours. But how can I say something comforting?

Do not take it so heavy. I tell myself that one shouldn't take oneself and one's fate as important. How many must die in this war, be it at the front, are at home due to air attacks?

Count myself as one more victim of this war.

With my estate, do as you believe best. I put all decisions into your hands.

Give to those whom I liked and who liked me, and those who have been nice to us with full hands. Give to the Dremmers for their caring for the children.

It's so good that I have all of you who love the children so much and will care for them. I want that you see them often. That they visit you and maybe you can go on vacations with them. Don't spoil them too much, though.

If they could live with cousin Fanny in America later on, that would be a nice comfort for my soul.

My dearest mother, I want to thank you for everything, especially for the life you gave me. It was wonderful, and I have lived it to the fullest and enjoyed it. Please forgive me all the sorrow I caused you.

Please see that my children will never forget both of their parents. We still love them, even when we're dead.

Goodbye. Forget all the pain and start enjoying life again - I implore you. I leave you now; you have to live on for my children. I have adored them more than anything in the world. Give them your and my whole love.

I will die thinking about my beloved Q, whose fate I share until my last breath.

Your daughter

Hilde

PS: Please greet all my good acquaintances again. I have thought about each one of them often. My best wishes to everyone. Be brave and look at life with clear, courageous eyes.

Hilde wiped a few tears from her cheeks as she signed the letter. She leaned back in her chair and thought about whom to write next. While her heart ached to tell Q how much she loved him, she would leave his letter as the last one.

She weighed the pen in her hand and stared at the grey wall in front of her. This cell was the size of a pantry and was equipped with a single chair and a table. Nothing else.

And what else could a person need who was about to cross into the beyond?

Her father and stepmother had been her pillars of support during those last eight months. They'd selflessly taken in both of her children and would now have to raise them as their own. Her heart was bleeding as she wrote her letter to them.

My beloved father and dear good mother,

Today, I must give my beloved sons into your caring hands forever. This is the hardest part for me, to have to leave my children. At least I know they are in good hands with you. I thank you so much for your help and your love for my children.

It would be wonderful if they could live with cousin Fanny after the war, it is Q's and my biggest wish. If this does not work out for whatever reason, then I still wish that the two of them always stay together.

Please do not let them forget their parents and always keep us in good memory. Let them enjoy every moment of their lives.

For myself, I can easily leave the earthly life because I have enjoyed my life to the fullest, and I don't have regrets of things I have done.

I go calm and composed, almost happy into my death. It shall be a consolation for you to know it will be fast and painless. Not many people can say that for themselves. We fall in this war like so many others, and you have the burden and the sorrow about our boys, but I'm sure they will bring you much happiness.

You also have two daughters who will make you happy, more than I did. Please don't take my fate to heart, and for the sake of the children, please look with confidence into the future.

Please keep my beloved Q and me in good memory and forget the things you didn't like about us.

I have always loved Dad and you, Mother. Even so, I have not always been able to show it.

Goodbye, my dear parents, Julia, and Sophie.

I'm your deeply thankful daughter.

Hilde

To my sweet little Volker and Peter. Your mother kisses you in her mind and while taking my last breath.

Tears spilled down her cheeks as the cute little faces of her two boys appeared in her mind. Exhausted by raw emotions, Hilde had to take a break before tackling her last letter. When writing it, she stumbled over her words, and tears dropped onto the paper, resulting in blurs.

Her heart was torn apart with every sentence she wrote, and yet she somehow felt the absolute confidence that their souls were interwoven for eternity and she would meet Q again – on the other side.

When she finished her letter, she called for the guard. He collected her last greetings, promised to bring her a meal and asked if she wanted to talk to a priest.

Half an hour later, the catholic priest entered the holding cell and introduced himself as *Pfarrer* Bernau.

"*Frau* Quedlin, is there anything I can do to ease your mind?" the priest asked her, seeing how hard this was for her.

"No, no. I'm good to leave this world behind, but..." she had to swallow back her tears before she could continue, "it's the fate of my children that weighs heavily on my spirit. I'm going to repeat history and do the one thing I vowed I would never do – abandon my children to be raised by their grandmother."

He placed a kind hand on her shoulder. "Don't burden yourself with guilt. Instead, be grateful your children have family who loves them and will keep your memory alive."

"I am grateful. I just hope that, one day, they will forgive me and understand my reasons for helping the Resistance."

"I'm sure they will, one day." The priest looked towards the door and then lowered his voice. "*Frau* Quedlin, I'm in contact with your husband and will give him a message for you."

Hilde nodded, tears filling her eyes. "Tell him I love him and death cannot change that. I will be waiting for him..." She broke off as sobs tore at her.

Pfarrer Bernau attempted to console her, but there was nothing he could say to make this any easier. He gave her the last rites and then left.

With trembling fingers, Hilde retrieved the tranquilizers her mother had given her from her pocket and swallowed them down. Her head fell on the table as she waited for them to take hold of her.

The executioners arrived some time later, after she was blessedly numb from the pills, and she followed them to the death chambers. Condemned prisoners were kept in a large cellblock building, designated House III, directly adjacent to the execution building.

She spent her final hour in shackles on the ground floor of the building known as the "house of the dead" before she was led across a small courtyard to the execution chamber, which was located in a separate two-roomed brick building.

By then, the tranquilizers had done their job, and Hilde was barely aware of her surroundings and was having trouble keeping her feet beneath her. As they laid her down on the wooden slab, she closed her eyes, bringing up the image of Q and her two boys the last time they'd all been together.

It was that thought, and the memory of Q's voice and Volker's laughter, that drowned out the sound of the guillotine blade as it dropped.

Hilde left this life, a half smile on her face. The Nazis might have taken her life, but they hadn't been able to take her soul or the memories of the joy she'd found in her family.

Chapter 43

Q finished another report for the War Ministry about inventions in the technical flight area, which in reality, were only variations on inventions that had already been made. He looked up as he heard the sound of the bolt and watched *Pfarrer* Bernau enter his cell. Given the late hour and the priest's serene face, something terrible must have happened

"*Pfarrer...*" Q said.

"I bring bad news, Doctor Quedlin. The worst. Your wife was beheaded this afternoon." The priest rested a hand on Q's shoulder as tears roll down his cheeks. "This information isn't official yet, so you cannot show your sadness to anyone. But I had to come tell you."

"This is all my fault." Q felt as if a huge millstone was crushing him to shreds. Despite him knowing it might happen, the reality of her death took him by surprise.

"We've talked about this multiple times. Your wife knew what she was doing and made a conscious choice to fight by your side. She wouldn't have wanted it any different."

"No, my lack of quick-wittedness and inauspiciousness was the real reason for Hilde's death. She was condemned because of me. It remains my hardest burden and biggest guilt that I carry around with me every single second of the day and night."

"Your wife has forgiven you, and you should do the same," *Pfarrer* Bernau said.

Q buried his face in his hands and murmured, "How can I forgive myself for killing what I loved most?"

"I accompanied your wife today, and she asked me to give you the message that she loves you and even death cannot change that." The priest folded his hands in prayer. "Her soul is now with Him, and she suffers no more."

Silent tears ran down Q's cheeks. "If only I hadn't let her type the letters–"

"There is no use wallowing in what-ifs. We don't know what would have happened. They might have arrested her on something else; the fact of being your wife might have been enough. The court was out for revenge and not for justice. We both know this. Loving you was crime enough to receive the capital punishment."

Q nodded, knowing the priest was doing his best to offer him comfort, but his guilt threatened to eat him alive. "At least I find consolation in the fact that I will pay with my own life for this mistake."

Pfarrer Bernau said nothing and simply sat with him for a while. When the priest left, Q slumped onto his cot, hoping to find the mercy of oblivion in his sleep.

***

Q spent an entire week in hellfire, grieving for his beloved Hilde, but forbidden to show any signs of sadness. Not even Werner knew.

On the seventh day, Q received Hilde's last letter. He held it in his hands for long moments, inhaling the lingering smell of his late wife. He caressed the paper as if it was her soft skin, and the tears started to fall as he began reading.

My dearest Q,

The time is here, and they have come for me.

My life started the moment I met you – do you remember the movie? Going Bye-Bye by Stan Laurel and Oliver Hardy. I remember you and Leopold as if it was yesterday.

Your love and devotion to me has changed everything. During those nine years with you, I enjoyed every single moment of my life. I love you with every fiber of my being, and my only regret is that we didn't have more time together. I die content because I had you and our boys.

Don't feel guilty for my death. It was my conscious

decision to stand by you, in good times and in bad times. We never took our wedding vows in front of a priest, but I always believed in the "until death do us part."

Q touched the paper where Hilde's tear drops had blurred the words. Memories of their wedding appeared in his mind. The matter-of-fact ceremony at the registry office. Misleading the waiting photographers with grimaces. The party with their friends and plenty of Hungarian wine.

He smiled through his tears.

I absolve you, forgive you for every action or imprudence that might have caused my fate. We were in this together. And without you, my life wouldn't be the same. So, in some aspect, I'm happy that I'm the first one to leave.

I wanted to live for the benefit of our boys, not for my own sake anymore. They will now have to grow up without their mother. At least I know that Emma, Annie, Ingrid, and our entire family will love them and do the best to raise them into good men. I can believe nothing else.

And, I pray that by some miracle you might still find a way to survive this war to be with them.

Sometimes, I wonder what might have been if we'd received the visa for America. But it wasn't meant to be. There was no easy way out for us, and I still believe we did the right thing.

This is goodbye, my beloved Q, but not forever. I will be waiting for you on the other side with open arms.

I love you.

Hilde

Violent sobs racked Q's body by the time he finished reading the letter. He crushed it to his chest and rolled onto his side on the cot, crying for the loss of his wife and their future together as a family.

A curious Werner turned around from the table where he'd been working on his novel, and one look into Q's face told him the content of the letter.

He walked the two steps to Q's bed and sat on the edge. "I'm so sorry, my friend."

Chapter 44

Q fell into a frenzy of activities in the following days. With Hilde gone, he felt the sudden urge to tie up loose ends and organize his affairs.

The first secret letter went to his cousin Fanny in America.

Dear Cousin,

I assume you have already heard about our memorable fate.

Also that we recommend our children to you if the aging grandparents cannot cope with them anymore, and the circumstances in Germany become too dire, and if my friends in the USSR are not available to care for them for some reason.

Because my wife's and my main motive has been the enmity to the National Socialism, you might be able to get help from your government to help you care for our children.

If one day you feel that the burden of caring for them is too much for you, please think about the fact that their parents died in their fight against an insane, inhuman anti-Semitism.

Live well! And if my sons make it through the war healthy and alive, please help them to make good citizens of a leading world empire, where they can use their abilities to the fullest.

Thank you from the bottom of my heart, and know that I will be forever in your debt for any kindness you show my children.

Your cousin, Q

He retrieved some of the money and stamps Annie had given him and waited for the shift of one of the guards who was known to smuggle secret messages out of prison.

It was a dangerous undertaking because the guards could get into trouble for doing so, and they required a *fee* for their services. Q could have asked *Pfarrer* Bernau, but he had vowed not to compromise another one of his friends – ever.

***

Q picked up his pen and started to write a letter to his mother. She had explicitly told him not to send any more secret messages, but today he just had to share the horrific news.

But he only got as far as "Dearest." For nine months now, it had been Hilde's name that followed. Now his Hilde was gone. Pictures of her took over, and he folded his hands and indulged in daydreams of a better time. It took him many minutes before he returned to the gloomy reality.

Dearest Mother,

Thank you so much for doing so much for me, I feel guilty accepting all your gifts. Also, my companion Werner Krauss shares his warm meal with me every evening. I ask you not to send me more food because you need it yourself.

Please do not send me more than a tiny piece of cake once or twice a week. With the simple food here, just some oat flakes, sugar, and a piece of apple make a true feast. I have learned to appreciate the simple things in life since my arrival in prison.

As long as there's enough dry bread and potatoes, and they always taste well, then any sweet is a sensation.

I fully understand if you or Hilde's parents don't want to write me anymore, now that my beloved Hilde had to leave this world.

Officially, you're not allowed to know it. The official enforcement notice has been sent to the closest relative, which is Hilde's mother, Annie Klein. I reckon you are not talking to her anymore?

Anyhow, I received her goodbye letter on August 12, but the fateful day was August 5. A good soul gave me the notice that very evening, and I had to live the whole week as if I didn't know anything. But I will write you an official letter with the announcement as soon as I'm allowed.

Please let me know if my two little sons are well and happy.

How did they and the Dremmer family survive the horrible air raids over Hamburg? We have heard worrying news, but I have faith that those two innocent souls will survive this awful war.

For my part, I'm prepared for anything. Anything at all.

I'm numb to the dangers and the horrors around me. My only consolation is the knowledge that I will soon follow my beloved wife from this world.

All the atrocities happening around us, those that I couldn't prevent, don't frighten me anymore because I won't be around long enough to experience them.

But you, my dear mother, wouldn't it be better if you fled Berlin and tried to find a secure place in the countryside? Perhaps with your sister?

I ask this for a very selfish reason. I want you to stay alive for a very long time to help take care of my two innocent sons.

With the utmost gratitude, I heard the news that my brother and his wife have offered to care for them, if worst comes to worst. They have enough on their hands with their own four children. Therefore I am doubly thankful for the offer. Please give Gunther and Käthe my dearest wishes and all my love. They are such good people.

Can you let me know if poor Otto was imprisoned as well? He was a dear friend of mine, and I always thought the world of him, but I never let him in on my secret, so I hope with all my soul that he was not doomed because of my actions.

Otto and I had opposing political views, and he never agreed with my opinions about Fatherland, treason, my fondness for Russia, and the communist idea. Nevertheless, I liked him very much, and I respected him as a scientist and wouldn't want to cause him to choose between our friendship and his political opinions.

It was a hardship to hide my inner conviction from everyone around me, except for Hilde and Erhard. But I could not risk anyone getting caught in the maze of the powers just because I wanted someone to confide in and lighten my own burden.

I will tell you, my dear mother, that day in and day out, I feel horrible guilt for being the cause and reason of the death of my wife. I have thought hundreds and thousands of times that I should have protected her better.

Please tell my in-laws that I suggested this very thing to Hilde (leaving her after a feigned fight), but she wouldn't let me. On the contrary, she told me she would stick with me in good times and bad times during life and until death do us part.

Her death has parted us, but I know that my death will reunite us forever.

My – our – life had become resignation and hardships, and therefore we decided to emigrate to America. My

Russian friends never tried to talk me out of it, even though it was against their own best interest.

The war is now turning cruel, also on the lightheaded Germans, who thought we were invincible. It is the difference in experience if you bomb the historic city of London with, at that time, superior weapons, or if you are now on the receiving end, enduring the tenfold of destruction by the now superior methods of the enemy.

In this country, the pain of others has never been important. There was no sympathy for their suffering. But true compassion has to be learned through our own pain.

This feeling of superiority and the lightheadedness/arrogance of Germany is coming back with a vengeance,

But I do not expect a rebellion of our people against the futile war. No, it seems that this time in history, the Gods have decided that what has begun has to be ended. Our country has to drain the cup of sorrow. Until the bitter and complete defeat, when everything in our beautiful country has been bombed to ashes. Only then may we arise again to become a better nation.

I do not envy those of you who will be there. No, I believe my situation is much more comfortable. A fast and painless end. The situation will get much worse before it gets any better.

Later, you will be able to calculate how little time was missing for my beloved Hilde and myself to survive.

Even our Hitler, always thinking of his ridiculous

ideas, will not want to survive a capitulation. He will not want to witness the formerly enthusiastic masses turning against him. He will search and find death on the battlefield, maybe even this year. In three months? In six months?

But you, my beloved and strong mother. Don't be a coward. Stay alive courageously and learn from events. Stay alive for many years to come and enjoy your grandsons. Help them with emotional support should the harsh fate of their parents tear them down.

About my financial affairs, please talk to Gunther. I am the owner of several patents together with Otto. I hope that the Reich, during the short time it will still exist, doesn't confiscate my parts.

It is my wish that my children will inherit the rights and the royalties.

As soon as you have officially received the announcement of my death, please go to the patent office and try to put the names of my sons in there.

If this isn't possible, don't worry. I do not believe that this Reich of a Thousand Years will exist for more than a few more months, and as soon as everything has crumbled to dust, an indemnification of the verdict against Hilde and I will be issued.

Then I'm sure Gunther will be able to receive what rightfully belongs to my children.

For you, my dear mother, it is my explicit wish that whatever money remains from my means and what you *might still possess from the envelope I gave you, shall be used for your needs as well. This letter is my testament; please keep it dear and safe.*

If worse comes to worst, I'm sure my Russian friends will help you out.

You have never stopped loving me, even when my opinions didn't match yours. I'm grateful for your generosity because I wouldn't want to leave this world knowing the woman who gave birth and raised me had stopped loving me. You have no idea how much this means to me.

One day, you might receive an invoice for about ten or twenty Reichsmark. It will say "for wine." Please pay it, these are debts of mine that I couldn't take care of due to the circumstances. And I wouldn't want such a minor thing as death hinder me from paying my debt.

I am in the process of tying up all loose ends, which I know can be agonizing for those remaining. If you want to know anything, please ask me. I hope I will still have some days of sanity left to answer your questions.

My moods are constantly changing. They are pretty accurately described in my last official letter. As you know, official letters must be much more careful than this one. We wouldn't want to cause too much work for the censors, would we?

As of now, I am well prepared for the "miracle of death" and not very vulnerable anymore for earthly sufferings. My suffering nerves are benumbed.

This is why I can eat and enjoy. At times, I feel an almost mystic unification with this world. Almost religiously, like you.

My beloved little mother. The one thing I ask you is to always remember me honorably.

This is another goodbye. I don't know of anything else to write at the moment. I have been writing this letter from eight in the morning to four in the afternoon.

Your – cursed by fate – son

Wilhelm

Chapter 45

On August twenty-third, Hilde's birthday, Q received permission to write his monthly letter. For a moment, he stared at the guard with disbelief at this inhumane cruelty, but then nodded and took pen, ink, and paper. The guard couldn't know.

He decided to write to the one person he had loved for all his life, and let her officially know about Hilde's death.

Werner seemed to notice Q's miserable mood and asked, "How are you holding up, my friend?"

"I couldn't be better," Q laughed sarcastically, "My sons are in the best hands with my in-laws, and I'm allowed to write down my research in the area of plant protection. What else could I ask for?"

"Freedom?" Werner asked with a shrug.

"Ha. Freedom is highly overrated. In here we have everything we need. No tedious household chores, no grocery shopping and the – admittedly bad – meals are always punctual."

Werner laughed out loud. "Well, if you see it from that point of view…we get enough sleep, have good books to read and even get to do some manual labor."

"See? The work they give us is even pleasurable."

"Well, I wouldn't classify labeling signs in a fancy type as *pleasurable*, but you're right, it could be much worse." Werner chuckled.

Q grew serious and fixed his eyes on Werner. Without his good comrade, he would have lost his mind months ago.

"I fully accept the right of my enemies to kill me, after the *chuzpe* I showed in my actions against them. And I die like so many others in this war, but I can say with pride that I have always been fighting against National Socialism and for a military defeat of Germany. My bad luck was being caught before the imminent end of war."

"At least you have the satisfaction to be in good company. In the best." Werner smirked and patted his chest.

"We all have to suffer the consequences of our actions, and I do it with pride. By now, I have had so much time to think about dying and how it will happen that it has lost its dread. Not many people in times like ours are allowed to die so quickly and without pain." Q sighed. It was true.

Every day at noon, except on Saturday and Sunday, he waited for the executioners to come for him, to be killed later that evening. But while in the beginning, he'd waited in deadly terror, this had transformed to angst, curiosity and finally acceptance. Since Hilde's death, it was like waiting to board the tram to reach his destination.

"By the way, my lawyer has told me that Hitler's idea of my public hanging in front of the Loewe factory has been canceled. I would have hated that."

"I guess you can thank our Russian friends for that. Rumors have it the government doesn't want to compromise their radio deception efforts with Moscow," Werner said, crossing his arms over his chest.

"Our goal was to make an end of this regime in 1942, but it wasn't meant to be." Q stood and paced the room, running a hand through his longish curls. "Not for me, not for you, and not for millions of innocent people on both sides who will continue to be sacrificed until some pigheads are finally smashed against the concrete wall."

Werner nodded. "At least we have the satisfaction that more and more people drop down from the praised ideals, despite the harshest sanctions and threats, until the unhappy end of this whole lunatic undertaking."

"Operation successful…patient and doctor dead." Q laughed hysterically and started shouting, "I do not regret anything! Everything I see and hear fortifies me in my conviction! This government has to tumble! The Nazi bastards must be defeated!"

Worried, Werner approached him and laid a hand

on his shoulder. "Hilde has forgiven you. You know that."

Q looked into the sad eyes of his friend. "I know, but..." Q sobbed and fell onto his cot. "Today is her birthday...I miss her so much."

Chapter 46

In the following week, he all but stopped doing his research work, and instead thought of ways to help those who had helped him by sending him money, food, or other necessities while he was in prison.

He intended to say goodbye to the world, and at the same time do a little good with his last actions. His situation didn't allow him to offer any material help, but the one thing he had left was his conviction against Hitler and everything Nazi. This he would offer.

Germany would lose the war sooner or later, and he hoped that after the ultimate capitulation, his status as a traitor of the regime might benefit those he cared for even after his death.

Q made a list to whom he would write a secret message.

From his three closest friends, only Otto was – hopefully – in freedom. Jakob had died during the *Reichskristallnacht*, and Leopold, a traitor of the regime himself, had been sent to a concentration camp.

Gunther made it onto the list, as did Hilde's parents in Hamburg. They would have to shoulder the main burden to raise two orphaned boys. Q's heart grew heavy at that thought, but he shook it away. Now wasn't the time to get sentimental.

His mother. Hilde's mother. At the thought of Annie, he hesitated. His emotions toward her were mixed. But he would write one of his "recommendation letters" for her as well, for the sake of his boys.

The good director at the Biological Reichs Institute and several of his ex-colleagues. Martin, his partner-in-crime at Loewe. Q smiled at the memory of how Martin had proved his loyalty. He'd saved Q from being discovered by spilling a cup of coffee over the classified material Q had been copying.

Then he set out to write the first of those letters.

Dear Friend,

My adored wife has been executed already, and I am eager to follow her. My two boys are well cared for with my in-laws.

And now the world history seems to agree with the opinion of my adored wife and myself about the Third Reich and its cataclysmic ado in the garden of God.

We die fighting the National Socialism. We hope all of you will survive the bad times, that will get all survivors into hot water, even though not without your own (passive) fault.

In the joyful certainty that this day is not far and that my wife and myself belong to the victims of the victorious side, I am greeting you.

Keeping this letter is dangerous. Please do so only far away from your own house, far away from Berlin, to be recovered only when Germany has lost the war.

I want to write down my plea to my friends in the Soviet Union, but also the other Allies, to give you and your family their benevolence, because of your good nature and your goodwill to me.

To whomever it may concern, I recommend the person presenting this letter as a technical expert, a good person, able to help in rebuilding this country, meant to work for the good of the nation in the future.

Prison Plötzensee, Cell 140
2. September 1943
Wilhelm "Q" Quedlin

After sending at least a dozen similar secret messages, he leaned back, pondering what to do next. Life seemed so distant that he did not even find pleasure in his research work. Since the prison didn't have blackout curtains, there was a strict no-light rule in place from dust to dawn. In early September, the sunlight faded into darkness shortly after dinner.

The next night, Q went to sleep with a satisfied feeling of someone who had organized his legacy, just to be awakened by the shrill noise of the air raid sirens.

Werner jumped down from the upper bunk bed at the same time Q heard panicked yelling from the guards and the other prisoners. He and Werner huddled beneath the table, pulling one of the mattresses around them in an effort to avoid being hit by pieces of falling plaster and concrete.

The hours passed, and the attack became worse. It was the most awful bombing they had ever experienced. A deafening noise indicated that several shells must have landed directly on the prison structure. Q coughed from the dust filling the tiny cell. The thick old prison walls shook like autumn leaves in the wind.

Another direct hit exploded somewhere nearby. Q ducked beneath the mattress and covered his ears until the smell of smoke made him look up. Torn open by the force of the explosion, the unhinged metal cell door swung back and forth.

"Look!" Q hissed. In the hallway rampaged a fire.

"We have to get out, or we'll burn alive," Werner yelled.

Heat and smoke filled the hallway as Q and Werner fled their cell. Many of the cell doors had cracked open, but others were still locked. Q heard the spine-chilling cries of agony from his fellow prisoners, begging for someone to rescue them, as the deadly smoke seeped beneath the doors of the cells.

But the guards had fled the cell block and sought shelter many hours earlier. There was no way to unlock the doors. Q cast a last glance backward as Werner dragged him down the stairs into the courtyard.

Shell after shell detonated in a blinding explosion and rocked not only the building but also the very foundations the prison was built on. The entire city of Berlin glowed with fire.

The Apocalypse had arrived.

Many prisoners in different states of shock gathered in the courtyard. Q ducked against the treacherous security of the wall, hoping – no praying – that the dropping shells would stop.

It wasn't until the morning light arrived that his wish became reality. When the smoke settled, Q saw nothing but ashes and debris where buildings once stood. A huge part of the cellblock in House III, including the adjacent execution building, had been destroyed.

Half of Berlin had been destroyed.

When the guards returned, they did their best to control the chaos and crammed groups of prisoners into the remaining cells. Q and Werner shared a cell the size of their own with four other prisoners. After counting and re-counting everyone, it became clear that four prisoners sentenced to death had seized the opportunity and escaped.

As the guards took stock, it turned out the prison had sustained massive damage. The death chamber was missing its roof, and the guillotine was damaged by fire, torn out of its underpinnings, it's operability questionable.

In the following days, repairs were carried out, and Q and Werner relocated to their original cell as only the door had been damaged.

Q couldn't have said what it was, but since the airstrike, a clammy tension had taken hold of everyone in the prison. The guards looked miserable, talking in hushed whispers while the prisoners waited in numb shock for things to come.

On the fourth day, Q noticed bustling activity in the courtyard. At least eight officials had arrived and were preparing – something. Leisure hour had been canceled for the day, and Q heard noises of construction work. He pushed the chair beneath the window to have a better view but couldn't see what they were doing. He reckoned they were working on the destroyed House III.

As soon as the night fell on September seventh, all prisoners were ordered outside for roll call.

"They're counting us *again*?" Werner tried to joke, but Q wasn't in the mood for joking. A sense of foreboding twisted his stomach.

It was cold that night, and the sky above the capital was pitch black, with the exception of the odd enemy firebomb detonating in the distance. Despite the blackout rule, spotlights lit the prison courtyard and their rays danced across the sky.

All prisoners were ordered to stand in file. Q took his place and then watched the spectacle in wonder, unsure what to expect from this highly unusual roll call. The tension was palpable, as everyone waited to be told what would happen next.

When the first eight men were called by name and led to the makeshift repaired executions building, a murmur went through the ranks. Several minutes later, eight more men were called out. The remaining men, including Q, stood in a stupor. Not a sound was heard.

Q closed his eyes. His time had come. He searched for Werner's hand and squeezed it for a moment. "That's it, my friend," he whispered.

Q stood there for a long time, while row after row of men were led away. He wasn't afraid or even nervous. The inevitable end was nothing to be afraid of. He even sensed a small relief that the waiting was over.

Once, the hangmen had to interrupt their work because several shells crashed into a building nearby. The spotlights went out, and only the half-moon cast the scenery into an eerie light.

The horrible murder continued until eight in the morning. When everyone was ordered back into their cells, Q didn't know whether he should be relieved or disappointed. He looked around, into exhausted familiar faces and nodded a greeting. A night standing still in the cold, waiting for death to come, had taken its toll on everyone.

Q and Werner had both survived and fell on their cots to sleep the entire day. In the evening, the same spectacle repeated – for five long nights.

At the end of the sixth night, Q and Werner were still alive. Q shrugged as neither joy nor relief settled in. After that many false alarms, his entire being was numb. All emotions extinguished like a candle.

In the evening, a visibly battered *Pfarrer* Bernau slipped into their cell.

"This…has been the most horrendous experience in my entire life," the priest said in a grave voice.

Q nodded. The priest was a good man. Having to watch hundreds of men being murdered must have been a lot to take in.

"Two weeks ago, Hitler complained that over three hundred prisoners were awaiting the outcome of their clemency proceedings and the Ministry of Justice promised to speed up the appeals. Which they did. In nearly every case, the sentence was ordered to be carried out immediately." The priest sighed and shook his head.

Q kept silent for lack of words.

"*Pfarrer*, you can't let those bloody nights destroy you. You need to stay strong and do good. The remaining prisoners need you." Werner had the ability to always find the right words, and after a few moments in silence, the priest showed something like a smile.

"I will. I will. I pray to God to give me the strength to continue."

"How did they manage to repair the guillotine this quick?" Q couldn't resist asking.

"They didn't."

"They didn't?" Werner raised a brow.

"No. The initial plan was to transfer prisoners to a remote location to face a firing squad, but the logistics involved were too difficult. Instead, they installed a beam with eight ropes in the execution shed..." *Pfarrer* Bernau's voice trailed off.

"Hanging?" Q grabbed his throat. According to his research, hanging was slow and painful.

The priest looked out the window into the sky as he recounted with a shaky voice, "The prisoners had their hands tied behind them and were forced to climb the two-tiered stool. The executioner followed them and placed the thin cord slip knot around their neck before pulling the stool from under their feet. The next prisoners in line, who were neither hooded nor blindfolded, had to witness the struggles of the others as they waited for their turn. In total, two hundred and forty-six prisoners were murdered during the last six nights."

Q stared at the priest, wishing he could unhear that terrible news.

Chapter 47

When the mass killings came to a stop, there was an eerie feeling of emptiness. From the original three hundred prisoners on death row, only fifty remained.

The guards seemed as shaken as the prisoners. None of them had witnessed mass executions before, and rumors had it that more than one of them had to be carried away unconscious and was later seen vomiting their guts out.

Since the mass killings had ended, prisoners were allowed their daily hour of leisure time again. A week ago, the courtyard had been crowded and noisy, now it was deserted and quiet.

Q sensed a different kind of tension in the air, and soon enough knew why. Word came that Italy had fully surrendered on September eleventh.

"Now the tide is turning," Q said.

"It was to be expected, Italy never had the military strength to oppose the Allies," Werner explained. "After Mussolini resigned, the new leaders did the only rational thing." He always had more information than most of the prisoners, thanks to his influential contacts on the outside.

One of the guards overheard them and joined their discussion. "On the contrary, Germany has lost a lot of ballast by losing Italy."

"Those *Itaker* have always been more burden than help," another guard said. "We really shouldn't have offered them to become our Allies."

Q kept silent, but he was positive that Italy's surrender was the beginning of the end to this horrible war.

The discussion turned to the horrific situation in Berlin. The air raids seemed to grow in intensity every night.

"Those child murdering Tommies have reduced half of Berlin to ashes," one guard said.

"I heard that most valued cultural possessions have been destroyed. Only a few precious pieces of art could be rescued in time and were now stored in underground mining facilities."

"To be honest, I'm sick and tired of this war. My two boys are fighting somewhere in Russia and my wife is a bundle of nerves."

"Our entire quarter doesn't have gas for cooking anymore," another guard complained.

"At least the city officials are providing meals for everyone three times a day. It's a bit of an inconvenience to go to the distribution centers, but our government cares for us. I bet the *Itaker* don't get that."

Q motioned for Werner to walk out of earshot of the guards. "Even when the entire country lies in rubble, the administration will still work, and they will still make one list or another."

"It's as much a virtue as it is a curse," Werner replied.

As they returned to their cells, the news of Italy's capitulation still occupied Q's mind, and he couldn't help but feel sorry for all of the poor soldiers out there. They were just men, or boys even. They shouldn't be out fighting each other.

"I often wonder what being in the trenches makes of a man. Gunther was in the Great War but refused to talk abut it," Q murmured more to himself than to anyone else. "Now his oldest son is a prisoner of war in Russia. His parents have no idea whether he's wounded or not. They are worried sick about him."

"There's rumors about the way Stalin treats the prisoners of war. Awful atrocities are happening on both sides," Werner said as he sat on the sole chair to continue writing his novel.

"I never thought humans could stoop so low," Q pondered. "Maybe Marx was right."

Werner looked up from his papers. "In what aspect?"

"There is no good in humans. They are inherently bad." Q stretched out on his cot and looked at the ceiling. The damage of the awful air raids was still visible.

"Why would you say that?" Werner wanted to know.

"Think of all the things humans have done to one another in the course of this war. Our kind has behaved worse than wild animals. We're no better than barbarians, and it seems the human race hasn't evolved at all in the last few thousand years."

"I agree that there's a lot of bad happening, but that doesn't mean all humans are bad." Werner furrowed his brows and smirked at Q. "There's you and me."

Q chuckled. "You're right, but we won't be around for long."

"Come on. If more good news like Italy's defeat trickles in, the war will be over in no time at all."

"God, no!" Q opened his eyes wide, as the meaning of Werner's words registered in his brain. "I hope the war doesn't end soon enough for me to survive."

"You would be the only person afraid to miss your own execution," Werner chuckled and turned to work on his novel.

Chapter 48

The year 1944 had begun, and Q was still in prison. He'd spent thirteen months incarcerated and barely remembered how it was outside.

Hilde's death had left a huge hole in his heart and soul. Five months had passed, and he still woke every morning with insupportable pain and went to sleep with tears in his eyes. Only in his dreams was he happy, because he was with her.

Not even Werner attempts to cheer him up worked, and day after day, Q's mind became more troubled. Like anyone else, he wanted to live, but not without Hilde.

It's my fault she had to die.

He had thought that same thought so many times that he had honestly started to believe that his rightful punishment was to die as well. Only then could he assuage his guilt.

Every day, he waited for his execution – and every day passed, and he was still alive. Deep down, he knew he didn't want anymore. Despite his jokes about it, this awful limbo between life and death took a toll on his sanity, and he wished the waiting would finally end.

Sometimes he whispered the words without wanting to, "Please God, let it end."

***

Q received a letter from his sister-in-law Julia with a picture of the boys. He stared at the picture, trying to manufacture the joy he'd always found in his children, but nothing happened.

The photograph had been taken on Volker's fourth birthday, and those two children didn't resemble the two boys that lived in his memory. It had been so long. Peter had been a baby – and now he was a boy. Try as he might, he couldn't reconcile his memory of them with the persons in the picture.

Q glanced one last time at the picture before he stashed it away. He consoled himself with the fact that they looked happy. *They are fine.* Then he locked up all feelings for them deep inside. *It's better that way.*

Several days later, a guard announced that he was allowed to write a letter, but it had to be written today.

The man wouldn't meet his eyes, so Q nodded and sat down to write…

My dear beloved Dremmer family,

By now, I am experienced enough to throttle down my emotions to a small flame. But this isn't the reason for my bad handwriting. It's caused by the old feather and not by my dwindling mind.

This morning, I was surprised by the announcement that I'm allowed a letter today and have to use it. Otherwise, the next possibility to send the letter would be in six weeks from now. But that is too far away to even consider it.

This is the reason I cannot wait for my dear mother's letter to answer it, but will take the opportunity to assure you of my love for you all.

While I'm still alive, Gunther has been made the custodian for my two little boys. I'm thankful that now two families, yours and his, are taking care of them.

Please tell my mother that I won't be able to write as often or as extensively as before, but that I'm longing for her letters and wish to know all the mundane details that you experience out there in freedom, and especially stories about the children.

There is an indifference settling into my mind, and the longer I must live with my death as my constant partner, the more it loses its hold over me, and I fall deeper into numbness.

We humans will never be able to fully fathom the wonder and miracle of coming to life every morning and leaving the conscious mind behind every night when *falling asleep, and finally when closing our eyes forever. The same way, we will never be able to fathom the vastness of the universe. But what we can do is to take away the mysticism and get used to it.*

And I, for my part, have had enough time, and I can say with some satisfaction, "I'm over it."

All the little things, all the thoughts you're sending me, are making it easier for me.

I've had several false alarms that gave me the security that I am not afraid to die anymore.

But this peace of mind is bought at the high price of indifference against human suffering out there. Nevertheless, I think of all of you in soft and distant love from far away over the clouds.

If you think of me and remember me in the years to come, be assured that I didn't suffer during this last part of my life. Know that I was bored.

For a long time now, I don't feel hunger or thirst. As I said before, my life has been reduced to a tiny flame. I'm fully aware that outside this life is not all sunshine. It is similarly constricted and unsatisfactory, surrounded by death.

The future is still a closed curtain, and as impatient as you may be, it won't be opened to anyone before the time is right.

Please take this letter as what it is. I have, in reality, not been there for you in a long time. Give my greetings to everyone, and especially my children, from a good friend who wasn't meant to be there for them.

I wish for my wonderful sons to be able to participate in rebuilding the world to a better place – albeit without their parents.

Yours, Q

Q sent the letter off with a worrisome indifference. Nothing, not even his research, interested him anymore and he waited to join his beloved wife.

***

Several days later, the guard arrived with news for Werner.

"Pack your things, you're being transferred," the older man said.

"My clemency appeal has been approved?" Werner asked with a hopeful smile.

"Yes, to five years of prison but don't rejoice too soon." The guard grimaced before he continued, "You're transferred to the *Wehrmacht* Prison Torgau Forst Zinn."

"A military prison?" Werner muttered, "But I'm not a soldier?"

"Every promoter of a seditious attitude can be interned there, including conscientious objectors, insubordinate personnel, deserters, those who aided the enemy, spies, as well as prisoners of war and members of the resistance," the guard explained.

Q looked at his friend. Happy and sad at the same time. He wouldn't be executed, but what would await him in Torgau? A place where few men survived the harsh conditions and illness that so often affected those incarcerated there.

"Well, this is goodbye," Werner said, putting on a brave face.

"Yes, goodbye." Q shook his friend's hand and then found himself engulfed in a tight hug.

When Werner released him and met his eyes, unshed tears made them glisten. "Be strong, my friend. The war is almost over."

"Take care of yourself, and one day, we will meet again in another world."

"Time to go," the guard called from outside the cell.

It was with both a sad and hopeful heart that Q watched his friend walk away.

Chapter 49

January 27, 1944

One month before his forty-first birthday, Q received news he would be transferred to the prison in Halle, a town about three hours from Berlin.

Everyone knew why people were transferred there.

"Is it time?" Q asked and looked around his cell, meeting the eyes of *Pfarrer* Bernau and the prison director who had arrived to bid their farewell.

"Yes. It is time." The director stood in the doorway to the cell and nodded with a sad face.

Q shrugged.

"Doctor Quedlin, I want you to know how sorry I am about this. If there was anything I could do…"

Q shook his head. "No, this is how it has to be. How it needs to be."

The director nodded, then turned and walked away, allowing the priest to enter for a final few words.

"My friend, are you ready for what is to come?"

"*Pfarrer*, I am. I am done with this life and ready

for what comes next. I'm waiting to be with my Hilde once again."

"I will say a prayer for you."

Q shook his head. "Save them for someone who needs them, *Pfarrer*. My soul is at rest knowing that I will soon receive the judgment I deserve and my Hilde will no longer be alone. Goodbye."

The priest placed a hand on his shoulder and then left. Q and several other prisoners were escorted out to the small van. A few minutes later, he was on his way to his final home on earth.

Q arrived in Halle midafternoon and was put in a cell on the death row. It looked very similar to the one in Plötzensee but without any furniture. Just a mattress on the floor and a blanket provided some comfort.

He raised a brow as one of the guards shackled his arms and legs, but his soul was too far away to feel humiliation or anger. Despite the further reduced ration, he wasn't hungry or thirsty. It was as if his body had ceased to function already. It was merely a shell holding his soul in place.

The minutes became hours, then days. A pasty mass of haze. Q lost all sense of time and place, the light and darkness of day and night the only indicator of passing time. He crouched motionless in the corner and waited.

Waited.

Waited.

On the eighth day, they came for him. In shackles, they led him to a room where pen, ink, and paper waited for him.

Q eyed the blank paper. He had said farewell to everyone he cared for a long time ago, and now only two letters were due.

Dear family Dremmer,

Today I follow my beloved Hilde.

I'm glad that the time of waiting is over and I will soon rest in peace.

The outside doesn't have any promises left for me, so much is broken. To think of a better future and long for it, is too far away and too foggy in my imagination.

Please make my sons' lives easy and happy. Today, the sacrifices are made so that tomorrow, life will be innocent and relaxed again. One generation had the bad luck to drown in the cooking kettle of our era, to give the next generation a happy life without problems.

At least we, Hilde and I, have seen the best of our time. When will it ever be so enjoyable as we found it in the short years of living together?

I don't have sorrows anymore about what I leave here on earth. Everything is in order. My help in rebuilding this destroyed world has not been wished for by the higher powers of fate.

It will have to be done without me, there are plenty of others, maybe not as understanding as I would have been a mediator between hostile worlds. But who am I to decide, now without me?

Q

February 4, 1944

PS: When you receive my belongings, please send a letter to Gunther. It's already stamped and includes a collection of spoonerisms. They may brighten the day of the ones coming after me.

Q paused for a moment and then took another sheet of white paper to write to his mother.

My dearest beloved mother,

This is my final goodbye.

Everything you need to know about how and why everything happened is explained in my previous letters to you.

Please do not mourn for me. I am resigned to what must now happen, and I will leave this world with my head held high. Soon I will be where I want to be – reunited with my adored wife.

Give my best regards to Gunther and tell him to live a good life once the war is over. May he care for you as I would have.

Know that I love you and cannot express my gratitude

for all the love and strength you gave me, despite our disagreements over politics. With time, you will see how right I was.

Your loving son,

Wilhelm

Q sealed both letters and left them lying on the small table. The guard returned with his final meal. Q drank the soda and ate the small piece of bread, chewing slowly and with great care. All too soon, he finished his meal, and the guard came to take him away.

The executioner was already waiting for him by the guillotine, and on steady legs, Q walked his way. Q caught the twinkling reflex of a ray of sunshine in the sharp metal blade and turned his thoughts to his wife.

I'm coming, my love!

***

Thank you for taking the time to read UNRELENTING. If you enjoyed it, please consider telling your friends or posting a short review. Word of mouth is an author's best friend.

Author's Notes

Dear Reader,

Thank you for accompanying me on this emotional journey through my grandparent's lives.

Most of what I know comes from letters that Q (Hansheinrich in real life) and Hilde (Ingeborg) sent to their family members. Unfortunately, the letters the two of them exchanged during their time in prison were never recovered.

The letter to Q's cousin Fanny in America (in Chapter 44) never made it across the ocean and was later found at the prison Plötzensee.

I took some artistic liberty with the person of Werner Krauss. He is a real person who survived the war and was indeed Hansheinrich's cellmate, but only for a few months. Krauss wrote a 33-page report about his involvement with the Schulze-Boysen group, which included several pages about his time in Plötzensee, sharing a cell with my grandfather. From this report, I have reconstructed their friendship to the best of my ability.

Pfarrer Bernau, the priest, was modeled after the Catholic Priest Buchholz and his Protestant colleague

Harald Poelchau, who worked both in Plötzensee and belonged to the Resistance.

The *Plötzenseer Blutnächte*, when the mass executions were carried out, happened between September 7 and 12th 1943 after a large portion of the prison was destroyed. Apparently, Hitler had complained about the slow clemency appeal process shortly before the air raids, and the destruction of many holding cells might have been the perfect excuse to speed up the killings.

It is not known why Hansheinrich Kummerow and Werner Krauss were among the few who were spared during those terrible five nights.

Not everyone in my family sympathized with the Resistance. In fact, Hansheinrich's mother wrote in several of her letters to Ingeborg's family in Hamburg, *"I am not sad about Hans death, he was lost for a diligent and civil life. Even after one year of imprisonment, he lived in such an illusion that he did not acknowledge the heavy guilt he had committed against his country. Our grandsons wouldn't have become good people with those parents."*

While Ingeborgs's mother blamed him for the death of her daughter (and told him so), his mother blamed Ingeborg for the fate of her son. But she never said so openly to the two of them, only in her letters to Ingeborg's family in Hamburg.

This is what she wrote in one of the letters in the possession of my family, *"Inge has endured the hard penitence, but Hans is still purging. One thing both my oldest son and I know very clearly now by the happenings in combination with remarks of Hans to me in the year 42: Inge has the bigger guilt at this tragic end to two lives. She has the bigger guilt about the final sliding onto the wrong path."*

I believe after more than seventy years, history had decided that they hadn't taken the wrong path in life. But it would take many decades to acknowledge their sacrifice.

After the war, the family was further torn apart by politics. Some of them lived in the part of Berlin that belonged to the German Democratic Republic, the rest in West-Berlin, and the Federal Republic of Germany.

Hilde and Q's good name wasn't completely reinstated for decades in the Western world because they had the "wrong" political reasons in their fight against the Nazis.

During the Cold War, it was unthinkable to commemorate someone who had believed in the ideals of communism and had worked together with the archenemy, the Soviet Union. This changed only with the reunification of Germany in 1989.

In 1995 a student of political sciences visited my parents' house to write a bachelor thesis about my grandfather. This was the seed for me to start challenging old beliefs and stoked the desire to learn what had really happened.

Thankfully, my uncle had collected all letters from that era, and I was able to reconstruct much of their lives and their personalities from those letters and other material.

Volker and Peter (those are not their real names) grew up with their grandparents in Hamburg, and both of them followed in Q's footsteps, as they went to University and became scientists. Each of them married and had two children. Me, my sister, and my two cousins.

I hope I have done a good job to honor my grandfather's last wish... *"I want to be remembered honorably."*

Acknowledgements

Writing this trilogy was a very emotional and at times tedious journey, and I couldn't have done it without help.

First of all I want to thank all my fantastic readers who've given me personal feedback or reviewed my first book Unrelenting. Without your encouragement I wouldn't have persisted to write part 2 and part 3 (in the works).

My terrific cover designer Daniela from www.stunningbookcovers.com, has once again taken my ideas and made them into a wonderful cover, that – in my opinion – captures exactly the mood of the book and the times back then.

And a book could never be complete without a thorough editor. Lynette Patterson has once again provided immensely helpful advice for the first draft, as well as found a thousand and one typos in the finished manuscript.

Many thanks also to JJ Toner who proofread the manuscript for me. He has written at least four books about WW2 himself and has proofed immensely helpful finding anachronistic words.

And last but not least I want to thank the fantastic readers at the Second World War Club for their unwavering support and their generous sharing of knowledge.

If you're an avid WW2 fiction reader, come and join our group:

https://www.facebook.com/groups/96208526720 5417/

Contact Me & Other

Books

I truly appreciate you taking the time to read (and enjoy) my books. And I'd be thrilled to hear from you. If you'd like to get in touch with me you can do so via

Twitter:

http://twitter.com/MarionKummerow

Facebook:

http://www.facebook.com/AutorinKummerow

Website

http://www.kummerow.info

Other books written by Marion Kummerow:

http://kummerow.info/my-books

93667458R00189

Made in the USA
Middletown, DE
15 October 2018